— THE —
NORTH EASTERN
RAILWAY
IN THE FIRST WORLD WAR

Learn more about Fonthill Media. Join our mailing list to
find out about our latest titles and special offers at:
www.fonthillmedia.com

Fonthill Media Limited
www.fonthillmedia.com
office@fonthillmedia.com

Published in 2013

British Library Cataloguing in Publication Data:
A catalogue record for this book is available from the British Library

ISBN 978-1-78155-081-6

Typeset in 10.5pt on 14pt Sabon LT
Printed and bound in England

Connect with us
 facebook.com/fonthillmedia twitter.com/fonthillmedia

— THE —
NORTH EASTERN
RAILWAY
IN THE FIRST WORLD WAR

ROB LANGHAM

FONTHILL

*Dedicated to Joe Woodcock, for without her support
and guidance I would not have been able
to complete this book*

Contents

Acknowledgements

I have received help from many people and organisations in writing this book, and would like to publicly thank them here. My main thanks goes to John Teasdale of the North Eastern Railway Association for his support and checking of the book for accuracy from start to finish, without whose suggestions and guidance I could not have completed it. My thanks also go to Leona White-Hannant of the Head of Steam Darlington Railway Museum for her assistance and help in my often very short notice visits to the Ken Hoole Study Centre, a superb resource for those wishing to study the railways of the north-east, and to the other staff at Head of Steam. The Search Engine research facility at the National Railway Museum at York has also been a great resource for studying British railways in general, again with very helpful staff. There are countless other individuals who have helped me, friends and family and members of the Durham Pals and Great War Society living history groups who I am also thankful to.

Introduction

The North Eastern Railway was formed in 1854 when four railways were merged together – the York, Newcastle & Berwick Railway, the York & North Midland Railway, the Leeds Northern Railway and the Malton & Driffield Railway. Other railways were also absorbed over the years, including the world's first public railway, the Stockton & Darlington Railway. By 1914 the railway's system stretched from east Yorkshire in the south to the Scottish border in the north, the Pennines forming the western border, with running powers and some lines running outside the main system area. As well as the railways there were also a number of ports owned by the railway, and also motor bus, charabanc and parcels van services. The east coast main line running from London King's Cross to Edinburgh ran through the North Eastern Railway's network and operated jointly by the North British Railway, Great Northern Railway and North Eastern Railway. As well as passenger services, coal traffic was heavy on the system, especially from the Durham and Northumberland coalfields – from the mines, the coal would usually be hauled to the docks on the east coast from where it was transported by ship. The coal and mineral traffic on the North Eastern Railway was larger than on any other railway in the United Kingdom.

When war broke out, the railway had had its most successful year in 1913, and 1914 was also looking to match or top the previous year's success. The war was to bring great change – 18,339 men were released for service with the armed forces, 34 per cent of the staff, and of those 2,236 were to die on active service. This left a huge gap in the workforce, partly filled by women. Industry in the north east was to go under huge expansion which meant increased traffic both supplying the raw materials to the factories and then delivering the finished products – forty-eight factories were enlarged and thirteen new ones built, four shipbuilding yards were enlarged and a further seven started, and three new quarries were also opened. This was countered by a large reduction in traffic to the ports on the North Eastern Railway's system, especially those owned by the railway, owing to German submarine warfare in the North Sea – this meant that the traffic had to be sent by rail instead for the entire journey, rather than a short journey to the docks. Coal traffic for the Royal Navy for example now went from South Wales through to Scotland for onward delivery to the base at Scapa Flow via the entire North Eastern Railway system, nearly two million tons of coal being carried in total until 31 December 1918 for the Admiralty. Troop trains were now a common sight, especially with large military camps set up at Catterick and Ripon. In total, until 31 December 1918, nearly twelve million servicemen boarded trains on the North Eastern Railway, 24,172 special trains were run, 134,208 horses were carried, 9,480 vehicles, and in total 5,524,989 tons of goods traffic was carried on behalf of the Government – only including traffic that either originated or terminated on the North Eastern Railway system and not including that which travelled on the system but started and terminated elsewhere.

As well as men, horses and dogs of the North Eastern Railway also served in the armed forces – as did various equipment of the railway: locomotives, motor vehicles, wagons and the rails themselves. The railway came under attack from the Germans by both sea and air, manufactured large quantities of military equipment including artillery shells (as well as running a new munitions factory built on North Eastern Railway land). The North Eastern Railway was the only British railway to have its own Battalion: the 17th Battalion Northumberland Fusiliers, and the reserve 32nd Battalion, were formed entirely of North Eastern Railway men, and although originally an infantry Battalion had their role changed to that of a Pioneer Battalion before they went to the front, and later in the war were heavily engaged on railway work for which they were of course well suited. I hope this book is a fitting tribute to all those of the North Eastern Railway during the First World War – those who went to war, those who stayed, and those who joined the railway during the war. Most of the information comes from the 'North Eastern Railway Magazine', first published in 1911 and continued to be published monthly until the North Eastern Railway ceased to be on 1 January 1923 as part of the Grouping of most of the British railway companies, and which provides a superb account of the happenings of a railway, a superb research tool for anyone wishing to study this period or look for information on a relative who served in the railway. Hopefully I have not missed out anything too important, and would like to invite contributions from anyone who has further information on the North Eastern Railway in the First World War for possible inclusion in a future edition.

Rob Langham, 2013

Outbreak

We must wait, we suppose, for the full story of the share taken by railways and railwaymen in the successful landing of a British Expeditionary Force on French soil without a single casualty. Meanwhile, the bald statement of the result achieved provides in itself a very noteworthy tribute.

North Eastern Railway Magazine, September 1914

There had been rumours of war for much of 1914 and indeed the years previous to 1914, the tensions rising between various European states, arms races between nations and jealousy over each other's empires being amongst the causes. The assassination of Archduke Franz Ferdinand of Austria and his wife on 28 July by a Bosnian Serb Nationalist set off a chain of events which resulted in what became known as the Great War. Germany's invasion of neutral Belgium to get to France and avoid the border fortresses on the Franco-German border brought Britain into the war at midnight on 4 August. Prior to this, in July all British railways had been warned that upon the outbreak of war they must be ready at short notice to put into force a programme of movements, carefully prepared already for the mobilisation of the armed forces. At the outbreak of war the North Eastern Railway, with all other railway companies in the United Kingdom, came under the control of the Railway Executive Committee, a Government body who would ensure the railways would run as smoothly as possible despite the great demands placed on them for moving the vast quantities of men and material, as well as normal services.

Invasion

In March 1912 an article appeared in the *North Eastern Railway Magazine* by C. A. Williams of York, describing a potential invasion of the UK by the enemy following a declaration of war. As far-fetched as this may seem today, 'invasion literature' was highly popular in the late nineteenth and early twentieth centuries, perhaps the best well known being H. G. Wells *War of the Worlds* of 1898, but most featured a human enemy, and more often than not either named Germany as the enemy, or a very thinly disguised Germany. The article was focused around the idea that shortly after a war would be declared, the enemy would shortly be on their way to land on the Yorkshire coast (again, it is highly likely that Williams had Germany in mind as the enemy), and had evaded the Royal Navy fleet. 100,000 men would mobilise in Britain immediately and head to Yorkshire, with the North Eastern Railway stopping all traffic, and York or Scarborough as the base of operations, with men and supplies being rushed through.

It is probably safe to assume that the NER management have in their possession a secret timetable that could be put into operation at short notice in the event of mobilisation.

Hull, which would be "a veritable 'plum' in the eyes of an invading army", Tyne Dock and possibly Sunderland would be made into coal depots and naval bases for the Royal Navy attempting to destroy the enemy naval forces – the author saw a precedent for this in the shipment of 7,500 tons of anthracite (for use in warships) from South Wales to Hull and Tyne Dock as an experiment. The loss of railway men for military service was not ignored – there would be a loss of large numbers of Territorials and Reservists employed by the North Eastern Railway who would be called up straight away in the event of invasion and their posts would need to be filled immediately. Ambulance men would also be useful in such crisis. He also forecast the need for ambulance trains;

There is also the grim side of warfare to be considered and the carriage department would have to undertake the equipment of hospital trains in which to convey wounded from the rear of the army inland, one of the first duties of an army in the field.

The North Eastern Railway would get to experience the transportation of large numbers of troops in a short period of time, as during the summer of 1912 the Territorial Force was due to have a summer camp in Yorkshire which would involve a lot of special trains needing to be run. The article was closed with the following lines:

> We all hope that such a state of affairs as mobilisation for war in Great Britain will never come to pass, but yet nothing is lost by a policy of preparedness. There lies in the heart of every Englishman a feeling, though probably dormant, regarding the welfare of his native land, and should our 'tight little island' ever be imperilled by an invading army, the men of the north would be up and doing, for if there is one thing which is dear to them, it is their liberty.

Life saving

On just the second day of war, an incident occurred at Beverley station involving an army reservist, on his way to his unit having been recalled to the colours. The reservist was drunk and jumped on to the rails from the platform in front of an oncoming train – Mr C. Franks, the assistant station master, jumped on to the tracks and pulled the man back onto the platform to safety, however the drunk reservist then turned on Franks and seriously assaulted him, leaving him incapacitated from work for a lengthy period. Franks was later rewarded on 12 October that year at the conclusion of a Beverley Town Council meeting when he was presented with a cheque for £10 and an 'illuminated address', both from the Carnegie Hero Trust Fund. The Mayor of Beverley who handed over the gifts went on to say that;

> Noble deeds are being done at the present time by both Navy and Army, but no more noble deed could be performed than to risk one's life to save that of another.

Further to this, Mr F. F. Lambert, a director of the North Eastern Railway, said that the actions of Franks and others that risked their lives for others 'spoke well for the spirit which prevails in England' and that 'the examples shown by the North Eastern staff in volunteering for the front reflected the spirit which pervaded the employees of the company'. Franks' death was sadly reported in early 1916 in the *North Eastern Railway Magazine* obituaries, too old to join the forces but serving till near the time of his death on the North Eastern Railway.

Behind enemy lines

One North Eastern Railway member of staff became stranded in Germany owing to the outbreak of the war – G. W. Pattinson of the Divisional Goods Manager's Office, Hull, arrived in Hamburg on Monday 27 July on holiday. The holiday was interrupted by the outbreak of war when Germany, coming to the assistance of Austria, declared war against Russia on 1 August and then France on 3 August. Pattinson and his companion desperately attempted to leave on the SS *York*, owned by the same company as the SS *Hull* which they had arrived on and was leaving sooner, but were refused, however managed to get on board the SS *Hull* once its cargo had been offloaded. The SS *Hull* with Pattinson and eleven other passengers left Hamburg on the evening of Monday 3 August, but on reaching Cuxhaven that night was ordered to weigh anchor at Brunsbuttel, the next morning leaving once more but stopped again at Cuxhaven, and ordered back to Hamburg, as Britain had declared war on Germany on 4 August. The Captain was understandably reluctant to refuse these orders – the River Elbe which they had been travelling down had plenty of German warships to deter them, and the sight of a British oil-boat, sunk by a mine, served as a warning. Once arriving in Hamburg Pattinson made his way to the American Consulate (the staff of the British Consulate managed to escape previously), told to buy a passport (passports were not necessary in the Edwardian era), and eventually told on 8 August that the only possible escape would be via Denmark, despite those trying previously being turned back at the border. In the meantime, Pattinson noticed the rapid change in Hamburg – signs were put up stating that 'Britishers' would not be admitted, and places with British or French names to entice customers rapidly changed the titles of their establishments – "The Anglo-American bar, for instance, became the 'Kaiser Kaffee'. After several other attempts at speaking to authorities to try and escape, Pattinson and his companion remained stranded in Germany with money running low, until late in August when they decided to visit the Dutch Consul and pay for an endorsement to travel through Holland which was marked on their newly bought passports, which meant they could travel through Holland safely. Saturday 29 August saw Pattinson as part of a party of five attempt to escape Germany via Holland by train and then onward ship – four of them had nothing on their passports, bought at the American consulate, to say they were British, however the fifth had 'a British subject' on his. The other four planned on pretending to be Americans to get past the border. The party had their luggage and passports inspected by the Germans at Bentheim on the border of Germany and Holland – the first got through without difficulty, however on the second person being asked if he was English or American, replied 'English' and was sent to prison – the same happening to the third person. Pattinson was fourth, and when the German official inspecting his passport murmured 'Americana', Pattinson echoed 'Americana' and was allowed to pass. The fifth person in the party was also allowed to pass, and so the three remaining reached Rotterdam following a further inspection from the Dutch authorities. He lost his friend in the crowd of people at Rotterdam and set out on his own for Flushing, where Pattinson boarded the ship *Mecklenburg* for Ostend, *en route* to Folkestone, where he returned to work at Hull and wrote an account of his adventures for the *North Eastern Railway Magazine*.

Workplace dangers

The dangers of working in Edwardian Britain were made evident on 24 August when J. H. Berriman of the Carriage & Wagon Department, York was unloaded timber when an accident hospitalised him. He died of his injuries just over a month later on 1st October aged just twenty-six, a sad end for a man described by his foreman as "civil, courteous and obliging and as capable a man as could be found". Work could be an incredibly dangerous place in 1914 and fatal or crippling accidents were relatively common.

Men leave for the forces

Upon the outbreak of war, the North Eastern Railway like virtually every other company nationwide, immediately lost large numbers of men who rushed to join the forces. First to go were the naval and military reservists who immediately went to their units or ships, followed by those who were members of the Territorial Force, the 'Home Army' created in 1908 to supply home defence units, and although there was no obligation to serve abroad, most volunteered to do so (many men of the Territorials were already with their units as when war was declared on 4 August 1914, the annual summer camp was in progress). The men that decided to join the army on the outbreak of war mostly went into Territorial units, one of those was H. M. B. Henderson, a trainee accountant at the Newcastle Offices, who had joined the NER in December 1913 and was on a twelve month unpaid apprenticeship. There were Territorial soldiers in his office, members of the Northumberland Fusiliers, and so he decided to join them on 4 August. He found himself "caught up in the flow of human endeavour at that time, and found myself in a drill hall joining the army the day after war broke out". Henderson joined the 1/6 (Territorial) Battalion Northumberland Fusiliers and spent the war on the western front, returning to the UK in 1917 where he was commissioned as an Officer, returning to the front in 1918 as a Second Lieutenant in the 2nd Battalion Cameronian Scottish Rifles, and in the Second World War would go on to serve in the Railway Operating Division, Royal Engineers. It was later calculated that by 9 p.m. on 8 August, just four days following the outbreak of war, 2,040 men of the North Eastern Railway were with the armed forces. Then came the turn of the civilians who wished to join, and by the end of August 1914 3,496 had joined up. September brought about the introduction of the New Army, also known as Kitchener's Army, which consisted of new 'Service' Battalions which would be part of an existing Regiment but only exist for the duration of the War, as Kitchener correctly foresaw a long, costly war, despite the initial hopes for a swift knock-out blow of Germany. Amongst the many Service Battalions were the 'Pals' Battalions, typically from the northern industrial areas, where men could sign up together and serve together. It was decided at this point that the Directors of the Company would investigate the possibility of forming a dedicated

North Eastern Railway Battalion, where men of the company could serve together, ideally the Battalion being involved in Railway work which was vital for supporting the British Expeditionary Force. Once the go-ahead was given for this, a circular was issued on 8 September to all staff requesting applications of interest for a North Eastern Railway Battalion. The story of the formation, training and service of this unit, to become known as the 17th Battalion Northumberland Fusiliers, is told in a dedicated chapter. Despite the rush of men to serve the country and the enthusiasm displayed by the company in creating its own Battalion of men, the only railway company to do so, the need for men to continue to operate the railway, which would be vital for war effort, was realised – indeed the same circular issued to garner support for the NER Battalion also stated:

> It must be remembered that a railway company has important duties to perform both to the Government and to the public. It is, therefore, necessary to say that the above terms will apply to men enlisting whom the company can spare; but whenever possible men will be spared and facilities given for their enlistment.

Even the small drawing office was affected severely by the amount of men enlisting;

> The North Road Works were working on their details for the duration of the war, when the call came up for volunteers for the army. Four of my men joined up thus leaving me with only four men in the office to keep the works at Darlington and Gateshead going with drawings. I had to take a hand at drawing again. As soon as I got my letters seen to I started at the drawing board and continued to carry on for four years in that way.
>
> George Heppell, Chief Draughtsman

Not all of the men that left the NER to join the forces went to the NER Battalion though – one of the most interesting members of staff to join the forces was William Wells-Hood, who was formerly in charge of the North Eastern Railway Road Motor Department, a position he had held since 10 January 1907. Because of his experience with the railway's large motor vehicle department, he joined the Royal Naval Air Service (RNAS) as an officer. The RNAS was fitting arms and armour to its support vehicles, initially to be used in the rescue of downed pilots when there were no set front lines, so it was possible for cars with pneumatic tyres to cross between the lines without having to run over trenches, barbed wire and broken ground. These vehicles developed into a fleet of fully-fledged armoured cars to support the Royal Marines and British Army. It was not long before Wells-Hood saw action, and in due course he would write about his experiences to be published in the *North Eastern Railway Magazine*, with accompanying photographs. His story is told elsewhere.

First casualties

Following the first news of North Eastern Railway men to die on active service, the *North Eastern Railway Magazine* opened a roll of honour from the October 1914 edition onwards 'in which to give brief biographies of North Eastern Railway men who fall while serving their country'. The first man from the company to be killed was Private F. J. Dale of the 2nd Battalion King's Own Scottish Borderers. Fred Johnston Dale had joined the North Eastern Railway in January 1911 as a motor-rulley loader, and as of April 1914 was a goods porter at Forth Station before joining the King's Own Scottish Borderers at the outbreak of war, with whom he was a reservist of twelve years. Dale was killed at the Battle of Mons on 23 August, the first major battle for the British Expeditionary Force in the First World War, when the British tried to hold the allied line against the German forces invading through Belgium. The Battle of Mons has gone down in legend as a checking of the German forces, with the British Army's superb proficiency with the Lee Enfield rifle causing heavy casualties against the Germans. Private Dale was killed aged thirty, leaving behind a widow and three children. He has no known grave.

Remount special

As well as the large numbers of soldiers and sailors being transported on the railways, another vast increase in traffic was that of horses

– especially trains known as 'remount specials'. 'Remounts' were civilian horses bought for military use and were purchased from all over the country, and would require bringing together at depots and introduced to army life. A remount special was described by North Eastern Railway staff member A. A. Leng of Leeds:

> The passing through of a remount special during the day may not strike the observer as being so interesting, but at night, the scene, with its glaring electric lamps, noise of hooves and khaki clad men, is one that cannot fail to be remembered in more peaceful times.

He goes on to describe how at stops, the soldiers would check for any problems with the horses carried in vans:

> Whilst it is being seen that the train is quite in order from a railwayman's standpoint, troopers with headlamps pass alongside the tracks to see that all is well with the occupants. An exceptional amount of kicking and disturbance in any particular truck arouses suspicion, and closer examination shows that a horse is down.

Sometimes it was discovered that a horse or two had fallen, and so it was necessary to remove all from the truck, and assist the fallen animal(s). Often they were completely fine and were just unable to get out owing to the other horses, but once back on their feet and their safety ensured, the others were re-embarked and the train would be on its way again.

Spy mania

The war had created a paranoia with regards to possible German spies in Britain, and both the public and military were wary of anyone who exhibited any unusual signs which could denote a German master spy at work, or just a North Eastern Railway Dock Office worker killing time, as happened to Mr E. E. White towards the end of 1914, recounting his experiences for the *North Eastern Railway Magazine*. After visiting a large recruitment camp at a location 'somewhere on the N.E.R.', he returned to the railway station only to be told that his train was not running, and was faced with a two hour delay. As it was a nice day he found an open, public, relatively busy grassy bank which overlooked the river and a busy railway bridge where he sat down. White had on him a small guide book on the local area which he drew from his waistcoat pocket and began to read. Ten minutes later he was approached by two armed soldiers who stopped opposite him. After jokingly asking if he was trespassing, he received the reply "Worse than that, sir, you must come along with us, as the sentry yonder reports that he saw you open a book and look towards the bridge'. Despite such a ludicrous explanation for armed apprehension, White felt it best not to argue and so was marched off between the two soldiers, a third then taking up the rear and then joined by an officer, who despite White's explanation and inspection of the suspicious guide book, told White that it would not be possible to have him released before the morning. Unsurprisingly the sight of a civilian being walked through the streets by several armed soldiers brought attention to him by the public:

> By this time there was quite a group of people looking curiously at the unknown and supposed "spy". It made me realise how easy it is to get into trouble nowadays and how careful one must be to avoid signs of irritation or resentment if still more unpleasant happenings are to be avoided.

After protests to the officer, a member of the Army Cyclist Corps was sent to fetch a more superior officer to investigate the matter further, and once he arrived listened to both White and the men who had apprehended him. After commenting on how the men had done the right thing, he was taken to the railway station where he was further questioned in the station master's office, and had his papers examined – however was then told;

> Your papers seem quite in order, but I cannot release you until I am satisfied that you are the rightful owner of these credentials; otherwise, I must detain you until further proof can be obtained.

As White was a stranger in an area he was not local to this may prove difficult. Casting his mind to a letter sent to the Commanding Officer at the Regimental Depot, the officer was able, by ringing the depot, speaking to the same man who had received the letter, to satisfy himself that all was correct with White's story and credentials by tallying the details and address of the letter and White's recollection of it. Following this satisfaction White was free once more after experiencing several hours as a suspected spy.

Rest and ambulance vans

Foreseeing the use of railways for mass-evacuation of the wounded, a few months after the outbreak of the war the North Eastern Railway quickly converted a number of goods vehicles for medical use. Two types were used – the first were "Rest Vans", 15-ton covered goods wagons which were designed to provide a rest area for soldiers or sailors feeling unwell whilst travelling along the North Eastern Railway's system on troop trains, and were statically placed at stations such as York and Selby and manned by the Voluntary Aid Detachment, a voluntary, civilian organisation set up in 1909 to provide nursing services to the military. These rest vans had a small number of beds and a dispensary for medicines and other medical equipment. Where rest vans were not placed, at other stations rooms were allocated for the Voluntary Aid Detachment to work from for similar purposes. The other vehicles were "Ambulance Vans", 25-ton covered goods wagons fitted with beds and stretchers slung from the roof – not for use as long distance ambulance trains, but for attachment to ordinary passenger trains to transport wounded from places on the north-east coast to hospitals in larger towns. These useful vehicles were converted at short notice at the York Carriage & Wagon Works, and to show their humanitarian purpose were marked with the Geneva Red Cross on a square white background in the centre on both sides of the vehicles, and were the predecessors of the large, long distance Ambulance Trains which were built by the British railway companies during the war, including the North Eastern Railway's Ambulance Train 37 in 1917.

The North Eastern Railway had for years ran Ambulance classes in conjunction with the Red Cross for members of staff to learn how to give medical help when needed – this proved to be useful both for members who joined the forces, but also those that remained in railway service and were involved in accidents. In August 1913 the North Eastern

Railway was involved in ambulance trains being ran on the system – for a Territorial Force exercise, which also involved Ambulance workers of the North Eastern Railway. The scenario for the exercise was that there was a war between England and Scotland, with the English army based at Richmond. The English force was on the march to Scotland when it encountered a Scottish raiding force at Berwick Hill, with a skirmish and casualties on both sides. In order for the English force to be able to pursue the Scots, the casualties were handed to the Voluntary Aid Detachment so that the field ambulance could accompany the main army. The exercise almost turned into farce, as due to heavy rain and a thunderstorm, those pretending to be casualties, even those supposed to be severely injured, soon ran for shelter. This withstanding, they were collected and taken to Ponteland station, a mile-and-a-half south-west of Berwick Hill. Here, the goods shed was used as a receiving station, and the casualties were transferred to a train of vehicles converted to carry stretchers, had beds, and also facilities for 'walking wounded'. The train then left for West Gosforth, where the goods shed had been turned in to a temporary hospital complete with straw beds. There were also horse drawn vehicles for transferring casualties to the Newcastle Royal Infirmary, the base of the 1st Northern General Hospital. Although there were a few civilian horse drawn ambulances, the majority were requisitioned from local businesses *etc.* and were of various shapes and sizes. The exercise was a success, and although an unlikely scenario, it was a good exercise for all concerned and hopefully taught lessons which would be used in the coming years.

Charity dogs

Since the 1880s, charity dogs were a familiar sight on the railway network – these were dogs that were based at large stations with a wooden box on their backs, into which passengers would donate loose change to certain charities, usually, and originally, railway charities for orphans of railwaymen killed at work. Since the start of the war, a charity dog at Newcastle Central station had been collecting for the Belgian and National Relief Funds and was photographed in late 1914 with Station Staff and Voluntary Aid Detachment Nurses on duty, either working from an allocated room or Rest Van as previously described. In October 1914 it was reported that the dog, whose name is unfortunately not recorded, had been collecting around £20 a month, a considerable sum.

Notification of Prisoners of War

Some good news regarding missing North Eastern Railway men did come back occasionally – J. A. F. Aspinall, the General Manager of the Lancashire & Yorkshire Railway, was held civilian prisoner in Germany at the outbreak of war at Munsterlager in Hanover, but was released fairly shortly thereafter. When he found out that he was to be released and repatriated, he made every effort to find details of as many other British prisoners as possible to give news to those back home. As soon as he returned to England he sent notifications off to their relatives, which would have been a great comfort as news of a loved one 'missing' all too frequently meant they were dead. Amongst the prisoners was Corporal Claud Edwards of the 18th Hussars, who was formerly employed by the North Eastern Railway at the York Station Parcels Office.

Gun trolley

A highly demanding challenge was placed on the manager of Gateshead Works on 30 August 1914, the first of many items for the war big and small made by the North Eastern Railway. Owing to the threat, which was soon proved, of naval attack on the eastern coast, an order was placed with the North Eastern Railway for a 54-ton trolley wagon to be built as soon as possible, to be mounted with a 9.2 inch naval gun for coastal defence. In peacetime it would have taken around two months for the railway to build such a vehicle – they were asked to build it in three weeks. All that the manager asked for was the materials to build it. The first materials were delivered on 1 September, and just eleven days later, well before schedule, the wagon was completed on 12 September

Staying behind

Working on the railways was vital for the war effort, just as vital as joining up for the Army or Royal Navy. However, those who stayed could be considered shirkers, not wanting to join up and do their bit, despite them on vital service. In order to protect its staff from unjust accusations, at some point not long after the outbreak of the war the North Eastern Railway issued official armbands, made of strong linen with a waterproof protective coating and a large safety pin to fasten them, with the North Eastern Railway badge surrounded by 'RAILWAY SERVICE' in large black letters, with an individual number stamped on each one. This would be worn when not in railway company uniform to prove the status of the man wearing it. These were superseded from December 1914 onwards by small, round enamel lapel badges which had a white circle in the centre with the King's crown and 'RAILWAY SERVICE' underneath, with a dark blue border with 'NORTH EASTERN RAILWAY' wrapped around the white centre circle – this type of badge was issued by all railway companies. Similar badges were issued by the Government and private firms engaged in war work to prove their civilian workers were undertaking vital work. Interestingly, the original armbands, which only seem to have been issued by the North Eastern Railway, came back in to use for female workers to show they were allowed on railway property, which would not be immediately obvious.

Wild trains

A small note in the December 1914 edition of the *North Eastern Railway Magazine* mentions a new 'horror of war' which would only have been possible in the early months of the war before a semi-permanent front line trench network cut railway networks – that of the 'wild train'. This phenomenon of modern warfare 'adds still another terror to modern warfare – this is said to be a train which is 'sent careering along a line at a high speed without driver or fireman' to meet the enemy's troop trains'. It has not been possible in the research of this book to find any documented cases of this occurring!

Water troughs

A more light-hearted subject than that of war and its horrors also appeared in the December 1914 edition – the topic being the phenomena of fish in water troughs. Water troughs were long troughs placed between railway tracks so that locomotives could pick up water whilst travelling over them, meaning they did not have to stop to take on water and were thus able to maintain a fast service. The water was picked up by a scoop which was lowered from the locomotive's tender. Although the fish were observed on the Midland Railway, it was still of interest to those on the North Eastern Railway as troughs existed near Danby Wiske and Lucker, with locomotives travelling as fast as 65mph whilst scooping up the water, which would lead to any fish caught up "undergoing a very exciting experience":

Many of the large railway companies have an arrangement of water troughs fixed in between the running lines of the railway whereby an engine may pick up water for the boiler whilst running. I was surprised the other day, when working on the Midland Railway, near one of these troughs at Melton, to see a 'school' of minnows, numbering from 50 to 80, swimming about in the trough. I wondered how long they would escape the 'scooper' of the engine, and what would happen to the feed pipes of the engine if they were not fortunate enough to escape. My fears were soon set at rest by a remarkable piece of strategy on the part of the fishes. The troughs are something like 400 yards long, and are refilled from a 10-in. pipe in the middle of the trough. Immediately on the approach of an engine at the far end of the trough the fishes swim to the drain, from which I may say they never get very far, and there waited until the engine had passed over, and as soon as they felt the inrush of a fresh supply of water they swam out again and waited about until they had to take shelter again. I noticed the operation take place for three trains, and was amazed at this example of sagacity. I may say that the water in the tanks is taken from a river near by which accounts for the presence of the fishes.

War changes

As the war progressed, some clubs and societies would be formed, others closed – the North Eastern Railway Camera Club shut down with the coming of war, and the following notice appeared in the November 1914 edition of the *North Eastern Railway Magazine*:

> It has been decided that, owing to the abnormal conditions prevailing as the result of the war, there will be no meetings this winter of the York Railway and Debating Society, nor will the usual prize essay competition take place.

Refugees

With the invasion of Belgium by German forces, large numbers of Belgians escaped and took up residence in the UK. At least two displaced Belgians were to work on the North Eastern Railway during the war – one was a Miss Julia P. L. Loonis of Antwerp, who escaped in 1914 and became a shorthand typist in the General Manager's Office, and another was a Mr Jules Crevecoeur, who pre-war was Chief of Service on the Groenendael-Overyssche Light Railway near Brussels. On 5 August 1914 he joined the Belgian Army, serving at Namur and Antwerp, and discharged as incapacitated in November 1914. He was sent to England, and started work on the North Eastern Railway in February 1915, initially working in the General Superintendent's Office at York until 21 June of that year when he moved to the District Superintendent's Office at Leeds, staying there until he was repatriated in January 1915.

Derailment

Late at night on 21 December a derailment occurred to the 5.30 p.m. Down express from King's Cross to Newcastle near Browney Colliery in Durham, between the stations of Croxdale and Durham. The express, made up of eleven carriages and two vans, was double headed by a 4-4-2 and 4-4-0 of unknown types which both joined the train at

York. At approximately 11.12 p.m. as the express was 200 yards past Browney Colliery signal box and travelling at 60 mph, the driver of the leading engine, John George Smith, noticed a loss of vacuum and immediately shut off steam and applied the vacuum brake, the train stopping 1,100 yards from the signal box with six vehicles of the train derailed. Curiously the first two were fine, the third one derailed, then the next five still on the rails with the rearmost five derailed, the four rearmost ones considerably damaged, however fortunately there were no injuries to passengers or railway staff apart from one passenger who reported an injured finger. The cause was found to be a broken rail, which had broken as the third carriage in the train ran over it, as the front bogie of this carriage was derailed but the rear one still on the tracks. The track that had broken was rolled in 1907 and stored until 1911 when it was laid, so age was not an issue and it could not have been foreseen. Extensive testing on the rail found that it smashed when dropped from height, so was more brittle than it should have been.

Christmas 1914

Despite the hopes of many (including the enemy) for a swift victory in Europe which would end the war by Christmas, this was not to be. The raising of what was known as the 'New Army' and would contain new Divisions and Battalions such as the North Eastern Railway was spearheaded by Lord Kitchener who forecast that this great clash of nations would last much longer than first thought, realising it would be a war of attrition that would not be ended until the losing nations simply did not have enough men or firepower to continue the fight. Of the 18,340 men of the North Eastern Railway that left to fight for their country, 2,236 would not return.

The Bombardment of Whitby, Scarborough and the Hartlepools, 16 December 1914

We are accustomed to reading about the shelling of towns by our enemies, but probably few of us really thought we should ever experience bombardment – our natural modesty would not allow us to consider our port sufficiently important to merit the friendly attentions of a hostile squadron.

'Bombardier' of Hartlepool, *North Eastern Railway Magazine*
January 1915

The urgent need and subsequent rapid manufacture in September 1914 of the 45-ton Trolley Wagon for a 9.2 inch Howitzer mentioned in the previous chapter to be used for coastal defence was not folly, there was a real threat of attack on the British mainland by German forces, and this was proved to the North Eastern Railway on 16 December 1914 when it came under attack by the might of the Imperial German Navy. To make up for the lack of ships compared with the Royal Navy which meant a large scale fleet to fleet engagement was to be avoided if possible, the Imperial German Navy planned to tempt smaller sections of Royal Navy Warships into ambushes where they could be defeated by larger numbers of German Warships.

The first attempt to do so was on 4 November 1914 with a raid on the coastal town of Great Yarmouth, which had the intentions of laying mines to disrupt shipping in the area, sink any ships encountered or entice Royal Navy warships into following them closer to German shores where the High Seas Fleet would be waiting, or alternatively to bombard coastal towns and make the Royal Navy disperse its Grand Fleet to protect vulnerable towns around the British coastline, thus making it less effective. However, after laying mines and firing a few ineffective shots at Great Yarmouth (which landed on the beach), two Royal Navy destroyers, a minesweeper and several submarines deterred the attacking force which headed back to home waters. However, fog resulted in one armoured cruiser, the SMS *Yorck*, straying off course, hitting two mines and sinking, with the deaths of 235 of its crew.

Despite being awarded an Iron Cross for his leadership of the raid, Rear Admiral Franz Hipper was severely disappointed with its effects, and on 16 November persuaded the Admiral of the Imperial German Navy to ask the Kaiser for permission for another raid. Following a U-boat reconnaissance of the Scarborough and Hartlepool areas for coastal defences which reported favourable conditions for a raid, permission was given to attack the Hartlepools (The Hartlepool headland area and West Hartlepool were separate towns until 1967) and Scarborough, the force consisting of battle-cruisers SMS *Seydlitz*, SMS *Von der Tann*, SMS *Moltke* and SMS *Derfflinger*, a smaller armoured cruiser SMS *Blücher*, four light cruisers and eighteen destroyers. 85 ships of the High Seas Fleet moved to a position near Dogger Bank, close enough for protection of the attacking force and to attack any Royal Navy warships that chased the raiders out to sea, but still close enough to German shores for protection. On the Royal Navy side, after the raid on Yarmouth Admiral Jellicoe was forced to split up parts of the Grand Fleet for coastal defence, however the Grand Fleet was still mainly based at Scapa Flow, Admiral of the Fleet Lord Fisher writing to Jellicoe on 28 November 1914 "You won't have a 'look-in' if the German battle cruisers come out, as they will hustle over and hustle back after bombarding, but I hope we will catch them with our submarines and our destroyers, but I see no way of preventing their coming to bombard, as we have nothing south to meet them. What a howl there will be!"

The Hartlepools were defended by two light cruisers, four destroyers and a single submarine. Scarborough had no Royal Navy protection. The Royal Navy had managed to capture all of the codebooks for the three main codes used by the Imperial German Navy from captured or sunken German warships, unbeknownst to the Germans, so when the raiders left port on 15 December 1914 the Admiralty was fully aware, and from Scapa Flow and Harwich large numbers of ships left port to ambush the raiders on their return from the raid, when they would be low on fuel and ammunition and the crews would be more weary. The force dispatched to meet the raiders would not be sufficient, however, to deal with the entire High Seas Fleet which was waiting to protect the returning raiders – exactly the situation Hipper wanted. Seven Royal Navy destroyers engaged several destroyers and the cruiser SMS *Hamburg* which were screening the advance of the High Seas Fleet. After the engagement, the High Seas Fleet turned back towards Germany fearing that the Royal Navy destroyers may have been the advanced screen of the Royal Navy's Grand Fleet, fearing a fleet on fleet engagement. Hipper's raiding force split up at the same time – all of the eighteen destroyers and three of the four light cruisers were ordered to return to Germany due to heavy seas. Battlecruisers SMS *Derfflinger* and SMS *Von der Tann* headed towards Scarborough to bombard the undefended town, with the single remaining light cruiser SMS *Kolberg* to lay mines off Filey. Battlecruisers SMS *Seydlitz*, *Moltke* and the armoured cruiser SMS *Blücher* headed towards Hartlepool.

SMS *Derfflinger* and SMS *Von der Tann* reached Scarborough and started their bombardment at 0800 on 16 December 1914, hitting the town itself, Scarborough Castle and the prominent Grand Hotel. The stationmaster A. Horsley was under the impression that "the enemy were making a raid and covering the landing of troops by bombardment and that our men were replying from the Spa grounds". It seems large numbers of the local population also came to this conclusion as, in Horsley's words, that in "'Remembering Belgium' they were in no mood to stay", with would-be refugees half-dressed and carrying all manner of possessions, including parrots, canaries and cats. However, at the station, the barriers remained guarded and tickets were checked as usual. Although with hindsight this could be criticised, and criticism was certainly raised at the time towards the stationmaster, this ensured there was no overcrowding on the platforms which could have resulted in injuries or even fatalities if people were crushed or pushed on to the tracks. The coolness and professionalism of the North Eastern Railway staff is shown by their reporting of the event – emphasising that of three trains due in, all but one was on time and of the three due out, only one was delayed due to awaiting the connection from Hull. That they were able to work to time despite shells crashing into the town around, with such an extraordinary event occurring that when they woke up that morning could never have possibly imagined, demonstrates a great deal of bravery. Scarborough's excursion station on Londesborough Road, built in the 1890s around half a mile before the main Scarborough terminus station to cope with the massive influx of passengers during the holiday season had its glass roof damaged.

After the bombardment at Scarborough, the two battlecruisers headed northwards to Whitby, shelling Whitby Abbey and parts of the town at around 0900. Despite the bombardment to the south at Scarborough, and a message reaching the North Eastern Railway station there with news from there, the staff had not believed it and Mr J. Birbeck the stationmaster had not been made aware, so it came with much surprise when shortly after 9 a.m. Mr Mawson and Mr Kinchin, the assistant stationmaster and clerk respectively, "had the unique entertainment of watching shells coming over the hill in view of the booking office window". Compared with the bombardment at Scarborough the one at Whitby was short, but still caused damage to North Eastern Railway property – a shell bursting near the station caused twenty of the heavy panes of glass on station roof to crash down, causing the entire station staff to rush outside. Light damage was caused to O Class locomotive No. 1786 of 1896, with a shell causing a piece of buffer beam to be broken and the Westinghouse brake pipe to be entirely destroyed. At Boghall signal cabin Mr Winspear, the signalman, only left his post when a shell burst six yards away, two empty cattle trucks receiving the brunt of the impact, shielding the cabin from more severe damage, although shell splinters were driven through its windows, also causing damage some distance away including smashing a wheel and fittings of a brake carriage. When he returned shortly after, when the battlecruisers had shifted targets, he found Rulleyman William E. Tunmore lying injured in the road. Tunmore had been in the company's Whitby goods warehouse when the shelling commenced, as he was attaching his horse and harness on to a loaded rulley (a horse-drawn flat wagon). Tunmore took the horse and rulley away from the warehouse, a likely target, to a place of safety, leaving the goods yard and crossing the railway line at Ford's Junction by Boghall signal cabin. Going up the road, the shell which forced Winspear from his cabin injured Tunmore when a splinter hit him in the chest. He was found insensible by Winspear and despite attempts to get him to hospital to try and save his life, Tunmore succumbed to his injuries before reaching the hospital, one of four North Eastern Railway men to die due to the bombardment.

Further north at Hartlepool, there were defences to fight back against the raiders. On the headland there were three six inch guns defending the large docks and factories in the area. Two of the guns were at the Heugh Battery, and one was a few yards south at the Lighthouse Battery. In addition to the three guns manned by the men of the Royal Garrison Artillery's Durham Territorial Force, a coastal defence force of the 18ᵗʰ Battalion (Durham Pals) Durham Light Infantry were on station in case of invasion, selected of men who had had practice of rifle firing on an open range – amongst the men of the Pals was at least one former North Eastern Railway employee, Private Les D. Turner. A telegram received at the Heugh Battery at midnight read 'A special sharp look-out to be kept all along east coast at dawn tomorrow, December 16ᵗʰ. Keep fact of special warning as secret as possible; only responsible officers making arrangements to know'.

At around 0800 a message received from the coastal Battery at South Gare at the mouth of the Tees saying dreadnoughts steaming north had been spotted, then immediately after another received from the Port War Signal Station located in the Lighthouse to say three warships were heading towards Hartlepool at great speed. It was believed at first that they were Royal Navy warships as they were flying the White Ensign. However, shortly after they hauled the flags down and hauled the German Eagle of the Imperial German Navy, and started firing out to sea at the four destroyers based at Hartlepool, the HMS *Doon*, HMS *Moy*, HMS *Test* and HMS *Waveney*. This caused further confusion on shore to the Heugh Battery who could not see the flags, and as the German ships were closer to the shore and firing towards the sea, it appeared that the Royal Navy destroyers were in fact the attacking German force. It was not made clear until the destroyers broke off their attack due to being overwhelmed by the superior firepower of SMS *Seydlitz*, SMS *Moltke* and SMS *Blücher* and turned their guns toward Hartlepool that they were the raiders. At 0810 the first shell hit – SMS *Seydlitz* had begun firing at the coastal batteries, one shell landing amongst the positions of the Durham Light Infantry, resulting in the death of the first British Serviceman due to enemy action on British soil during the First World War, Private Theo Jones of the

Durham Pals. Another shell killed more Durham Pals, including Private Les D. Turner, service number 18/398 of 'Dalmeny', 10 Rectory Drive, Gosforth. He had worked as a clerk at the Divisional Superintendent's Office in Newcastle before joining the Pals in September 1914, and was twenty-four years old when he was killed. The men of the Heugh and Lighthouse Batteries were not simply taking cover, they were fighting back – they immediately engaged the German ships, the third round hitting SMS *Seydlitz*, killing nine seamen, injuring three others. Further direct hits were achieved on the battlecruiser, before all three of the raiders were now firing complete broadsides into the Batteries. Fortunately for the defenders, owing to the sloping nature of the ground in front of the batteries, many of the shells ricocheted and exploded over the top of the battery, or hit the cliffs or promenade below. If they were aimed slightly too high, the shells would fly over the top of the battery but drop down into the town below and behind. Hartlepool's remaining defending force attempted to put to sea, the light cruiser HMS *Patrol* going full steam ahead out of the harbour hoping to avoid the barrage of shells falling between the harbour and the sea. Unfortunately, just as it was leaving the armoured cruiser SMS *Blücher* came into view and was immediately fired upon, and then by the two battlecruisers once seen. Severely damaged, the captain of HMS *Patrol* had no choice but to run aground to avoid further casualties. This blocked the channel preventing HMS *Forward* from leaving and engaging the raiders. The submarine, C9, managed to dive to escape shells and put out to sea, but was unable to position itself to attack the raiders.

After the failed attempt to silence the defences (the coastal batteries continued to fire upon the ships throughout the bombardment) both battlecruisers gave their full attention to West Hartlepool, concentrating on industrial sites, including the railway station and network which the North Eastern Railway had built up in the area. At West Hartlepool station, shortly after the Liverpool service departed a shell smashed through the station wall at the south end of the 'up' platform. The same shell damaged the brake of the train due out at 0850, and the passenger line to the south was cut in several places. After the first fifteen minutes of the bombardment by 0830 the staff left the station to ensure the safety of their families, but returned shortly afterwards to continue operating.

At Hartlepool station only four staff plus the stationmaster were working at the time of the bombardment. Mr Walker, a ticket collector, gave first aid to a sailor on the SS *Phoebe* in dock close to the station, who had been mortally wounded by shrapnel. Mr Llewellyn, a porter, made stretcher and ambulance materials ready, and Mr Willey, also a porter, gathered women into the waiting rooms away from the falling glass due to shell fire. Despite the chaos around them, it was noted by one member of staff that "there was no excitement at all, not even amongst the passengers". In the docks, despite the heavy bombardment of the area shunters and engine drivers of the North Eastern Railway stayed at their posts working as usual until it became too dangerous to continue. In many places the rails were cut by shells or blocked by debris. Railway operations for the rest of the day were mainly disrupted by both the damage to portions of track and damage to telegraph wires.

Aside from Private Les D. Turner at the Heugh Battery, two other North Eastern Railway men were killed in the bombardment at the Hartlepools. George Dring, a mooringman, was wounded in the chest by a piece of shell and died later in the day. With around a dozen others he had taken shelter behind the dockmaster's offices. A shell struck one of the crabwinches which controlled the dock gates, smashing it, wounding six or seven men and killing four, including George Dring. Dring was born in 1867 and spent fourteen years as a merchant sailor until he joined the North Eastern Railway in 1894, originally working on a dock dredger used by the Dock Engineer's Department. In 1904 he was appointed to the position of mooringman (a Dock Pilot) in the Dockmaster's Department which he held until his death. He was known as a quiet and well conducted man, highly regarded by those he worked with, and left a widow and six sons and daughters, two of whom were still at school when he was killed.

William Sarginson, a shunter at West Hartlepool, was the second NER casualty. He was working at Slag Island in the dock area at during the bombardment, and continued to deal with wagons during the shelling despite the obvious danger. Fragments of a shell which hit the docks injured Sarginson, and he called out to his mate Mr R. Coates to help him. Coates carried him away on his back to shelter and help when another shell hit, fragments injuring both of the men, resulting on over twenty individual wounds to parts of his body by the time he got to hospital. Unfortunately he died in hospital on 4

January 1915 owing to his wounds at twenty-two years old. He had been employed with the North Eastern Railway since June 1913 and was well liked.

The raid on Hartlepool finally ended with the last shell being fired by the raiders at 0850. The raid had been planned to last a full hour, but had been cut down to forty minutes owing to the constant shelling from the three six inch guns on the Headland. Around 127 civilians, nine military men and four Royal Navy men were killed in total during the Hartlepools Bombardment, and over 400 injured, likely nearer 500, and not including very lightly wounded who would have looked after themselves. Eighteen were killed at Scarborough and seven at Whitby, and in total almost 600 across all three towns were wounded (127 deaths from the raid on the Hartlepools comes from a 1916 newspaper report, and there could have been more – 110 is widely accepted and was the 1918 official figure however casualties died of wounds in hospitals well into 1915 due to infections and possibly beyond, and there were at least two suicides due to the raid also). As well as the damage to the North Eastern Railway already mentioned, wagons and equipment in the docks area were also heavily damaged – a pair of 100 ton sheer legs had one steel leg pierced by shell, and on a weighing machine the wire ropes and sheaves were shot away causing the machine to fall and be 'utterly destroyed'. There was also damage by shell fragments to a coal elevator, an electric crane and a steam crane. A parachute water column was also damaged and a glancing shell caused damage to the North Eastern Railway owned power station chimney. At West Hartlepool engine shed two locomotives were damaged – No. 553, an L Class 0-6-0T engine designed for use in the docks area had a bulge in the smoke box side and a small hole in the dome case and front lagging sheet, and No. 571, a 59 Class 0-6-0 tender engine of 1884 had two small holes in the cab side and two holes through the tank side, both repaired in January 1915 and put back into service. The coaling stage had one corner broken off and three holes blown through the front wall, as well as a ridge tile being knocked off. The engine shed itself had a hole through the roof slates and boarding damaged. At Slag Island in West Hartlepool a parachute tank was pierced with a valve rod broken and decking damaged. More minor damage includes a railway bench hit by a shell – one of the large, cast iron 'feet' of the bench being blown vertically into the air and falling right down a nearby house's chimney ending up in the fireplace. Some railway sleepers hit by a shell were thrown into the gates of a large building known as 'The Willows' on the headland.

Following the raid, on 18 June 1915, thirty-four members of North Eastern Railway local ambulance classes were given medals by General Manager Sir A. Kaye Butterworth for distinguishing themselves under fire during the bombardment. After the 18 June presentation it was discovered that two ticket collectors had also rendered special services but had escaped official recognition. Sir Alexander agreed these men should have medals obtained for them also, and the two men, Mr James P. Devlin and Mr James Walker were presented with the medals by General Superintendent Major H. A. Watson on 21 September 1915.

1915

By the start of 1915 the trenches had been established on the western front from the Belgian coast to the Swiss border. There was a hope of knocking Germany out of the war by capturing Constantinople and forcing the Ottoman Empire to surrender – following a failed attempt to force the Dardanelles with ships, a multi-national amphibious landing on the Gallipoli peninsula took place. The Gallipoli campaign was also a failure, a waste of soldiers from Britain, France, Australia, New Zealand and elsewhere who would have been better employed on the Western Front. The Second Battle of Ypres saw the British forces subjected to mass gas attacks shortly after its first use in warfare against the Russians. The Battle of Loos commenced in late September, it was hoped to use large numbers of bombs to blast a way through the German lines – the primitive bombs mostly failed owing to wet conditions. On 7 May the civilian British liner RMS Lusitania was sunk without warning by a German submarine with the massive loss of life of 1,195 passengers and crew, including 128 Americans, causing outrage. Zeppelins started to bomb Britain, focusing on London, terrorising British civilians for much of the rest of the war. On 22 May at Quintinshill, Scotland a troop train carrying the 1/7th Battalion Royal Scots on their way to Gallipoli collided with a local passenger train – an express train ran into the wreckage around a minute later as rescue efforts were underway. Fire spread rapidly and ferociously by the gas lighting used for the carriages and soon engulfed the wreckage of the three trains involved and two goods trains standing nearby – with a death toll of around 226 (the total figure was never confirmed, *as the Battalion's roll was destroyed in the disaster), Quintinshill was and still is Britain's most deadly railway disaster.*

North Eastern Railway tug and eight men are lost

On 16 January 1915, off the coast of Deal, Kent, former North Eastern Railway steam tug *Stranton*, now under the name of HMS *Char*, went to the assistance of the *Frivan* a Belgian vessel which was in distress. HMS *Char* was standing off to inspect the *Frivan* when a large sea drove her across *Frivan*'s bows, holing and quickly sinking her, with the loss of all hands. *Stranton*, built for the North Eastern Railway in 1899 and based at West Hartlepool, had previous history of receiving damage when assisting vessels in need. On 8 May 1913, *Stranton* went to the aid of a Swedish barque *Meda* which had broken free from her mooring ropes at Hartlepool docks and grounded where it looked like she would surely be wrecked. Whilst the *Meda* was drifting, the North Eastern Railway crew of the *Stranton* made many attempts to throw lines to the helpless crew. Then the two propellers of the *Stranton* struck an unknown obstacle, almost entirely stripping them and making *Stranton* just as useless as *Meda*, and she began to drift too, the would-be rescuer now in need of rescue herself. Hartlepool's RNLI lifeboat arrived on scene and took off the crew of both the *Meda* and the *Stranton*, however not without difficulty;

> A second visit had to be made to the '*Stranton*' before the men could be induced to leave and then they only did so on the advice of Captain Standing, Assistant Dock Master, who accompanied the Lifeboat. Captain J Whales, of the *Stranton*, elected to remain on board and did so despite the danger.

Eventually the *Stranton* drifted up Middleton Beach and when the tide receded was left clear out of the water, the severe damage to her propellers becoming apparent. The *Stranton* was floated soon after and towed to Newcastle where she was repaired and re-entered service at West Hartlepool. The tug was hired by the Admiralty on 17 November 1914, the entire eight man crew volunteering to join the Royal Navy and continuing to serve with the her, all of them perishing when she sank following the collision with the *Frivan*, along with nine further Royal Navy men. The North Eastern Railway men drowned were:

E. Booth, fireman (formerly deck hand)
W. Booth, artificer (formerly engineer)
R. Fergus, petty officer (formerly mate)
M. Hastings, able seaman (formerly deck hand)
W. Hatch, fireman (same role as in North Eastern Railway service)
J. E. Hunter, fireman (same role as in North Eastern Railway service)
G. Nossiter, artificer (formerly second engineer)
J. P. Whale, lieutenant (captain in command of HMS *Char*, formerly master)

The loss of the tug and her entire peacetime North Eastern Railway crew understandably came as a blow to the company, especially to those at Hartlepool following the deaths of men and destruction caused owing to the German fleet exactly a month previously.

Changing railway scene

The large numbers of servicemen travelling on the railways brought a big change to the railway scene, and a fascinating insight into what it was like to work in a typical railway booking office during the war was written by A. A. Leng of Leeds Station in early 1915:

> At the present time through a booking office window a student of humanity can find much to interest him. The booking of military men has come to be regarded as quite a special section. Recruits, trained soldiers, and often, alas, men broken in the war, have all to be catered for.
>
> The recruits are particularly interesting. The majority seem fully to realise the step they are taking, and present their warrants, entitling them to free tickets in business-like fashion. A few, but only a few, celebrate their departure by partaking too freely of the cup that cheers, and on arrival at the office have but a hazy idea of where and when they intend to travel. Much can, however, be excused, and they are strictly enjoined to take great care of their ticket.

The soldier on furlough is a familiar figure. Full of joy at the prospect of seeing those dear to him, he appears at the window with smiling face, and it is a pleasure to help him on his journey.

A rather pathetic sight is afforded by those who have been wounded, and are going from hospital to some convalescent home, while at times, men hand in warrants bearing the information that they are being discharged as unfit for further military service. They have done their share for the Empire. That there is a tremendous number of army forms and documents is well known, and it is often the task of the booking clerk to instruct the soldier which form he has to give up in exchange for a ticket. Some insist on handing over their pass authorising them to be absent from barracks, and without which they are liable to arrest on sight by the military police, and recruits sometimes give in the form containing all personal particulars of themselves – height, colour of hair, religion, &c.

A stranger to railway work who happens to be standing behind the window when a commanding voice proclaims that 100 men are to travel by a train due to depart in a few minutes may imagine that the ever-ready clerk is to be cornered at last, but one ticket suffices for the whole party, and is supplied in a moment. In addition to the ordinary soldier, the officer is a constant client. Sufficient to say, in respect to this class, that it is composed of ideal English gentlemen.

A booking office is also kept very much occupied in these days in answering inquiries by people who wish to travel to visit their husbands, sons, or sweethearts, stationed in other towns. Many are of the poorer classes, and much patience is needed to instil into them the desired information. Very often the mention of the fare to a place far distant brings a look of disappointment to their faces.

A remarkable development of modern warfare is the case with which a soldier can travel home to see his friends, or with which they can get to see him. The limit is reached when men are even granted week-end leave from the firing line itself. In the olden days, if a man were going to the war it meant his absence from home for years, and the changed conditions must be regarded as another triumph achieved by railway transport.

Another viewpoint was later provided in another issue, that of the Marshalling Yard, by A. L. Stead, but the location was not given, understandably as it described what would make a very tempting enemy target:

Clank! Clank! Clank! It demands skilled hands to couple up quickly the string of trucks lying in the siding. The regularity with which the sound is repeated is evidence of man's dexterity. Had you felt disposed to count the times the musical sound of coupling meeting hook rang out, you might have calculated the length of the train as about 50 wagons. And this is but a very small fraction of the night's work. The occupants of the neighbouring cottages, whose rest must surely be disturbed by the constant noise, probably do not regard the nocturnal shunting operations with quite the same degree of enthusiasm as the railwayman; maybe the weary householder, vainly wooing repose, will express the extent of the night's work on the line in terms of so many well-earned rest denied him. On the other hand, the more disturbed his sleep, the larger number of entries appear on the shunters' reports in the morning, and, uncharitable though it may seem, the more the train foreman will rub his hands in satisfaction.

In the day-time, passers-by have always been attracted by the noise and bustle arising out of the conduct of operations in the yard. The children of the district, in particular, must have spent many happy hours watching the work being carried out, eyes open wide to catch every movement of locomotive or vehicle. One or two, more absorbed than their fellows, may even unthinkingly have awarded the study of railway operating priority of place to school lessons, and received due punishment for the crime on their awakening.

But recently added interest has been given to the pastime. Possession of a point of vantage on a conveniently situated boundary wall running alongside the line, from which to view the scene, is now difficult to obtain. Curiously-printed labels and lettering on wagon sides were noticed and remarked upon by observant onlookers. At first it was "Government Stores – Urgent" and "Foodstuffs – Perishable," which gave the hint of something unusual astir. The arrival and departure of long, low trucks, conveying huge, white-painted castings, was noted with pleasure. One day a train-load of natty two-wheeled carts, on which were fitted alongside each other a couple of metal cylinders, provided food for thought – and much chatter; later, a stray illustration appearing on the back page of the local newspaper revealed their purpose, and the "ammunition wagon" theory advanced by one bright youngster fell through. Eventually a boy, more daring than the rest, ventured a short distance along the top of the embankment which hid a portion of the yard from view. And there, at the foot of the slope, he saw "them" for the first time – half-a-dozen stoutly-built steel trucks lettered with "Gunpowder." His happiness was complete. No longer was "war" something vague, unimaginable and remote, being conducted in a strange country far across the water; there it was, not 20 yards distant, cooped up in those awe-compelling black vans.

Tragedy at Scarborough

The dangers of working on the railways in the days of steam were made apparent after a tragic accident on 17 March near Scarborough station at around 8.00 p.m., involving the 6.38 p.m. Whitby to Scarborough passenger train. Owing to the position of Scarborough station and the railway line from Whitby running to it, it was necessary when a station pilot (a locomotive based at a station to aid in positioning trains or other general purposes) was not available for the train to stop, and the locomotive run around the train and attach to the rear to pull the train into Scarborough station. The normal procedure was for the carriages to stand on the middle road between Falsgrave and Washbeck signal boxes, and the locomotive run around using the Scarborough excursion station platform line. Whilst this was being done, the guard would leave the train and move the lamp at the rear of the train to what had previously been the front of the train. In total there were six minutes allowed for this operation, and so locomotive crews also sometimes found it necessary for the fireman, who would need to leave the locomotive anyway to uncouple the locomotive from the train and then couple it at the other end, to simply remain off the locomotive whilst it ran round to save time.

The driver of the 0-4-4T locomotive was John William Smith, a frequent driver on the route and so was highly familiar with the operation. Unfortunately, as he was running the locomotive around the train, consisting of three carriages, he struck the train at between four and five miles per hour. The locomotive was on the same line as the train, instead of the adjacent line, and collided with the train it had recently become uncoupled from. He found the guard of the train lying on the ground, killed instantaneously, with the lamp lying on the tracks, and the fireman severely injured, so much so that he was unable to attend the inquiry several weeks later. Five passengers also notified the North Eastern Railway of slight injury, and there was damage to the locomotive and carriage it struck too. The railway points were controlled by Washbeck signal box, in the charge of Signalman William Bielby, however it was found that the Signal Lad, John Henry Smith who was a boy employed only to answer the telephone and write in the book, had on occasion been using the levers which controlled the points and signals under Bielby's instruction and strict observation, and had done the operation for the Whitby to Scarborough train about half a dozen times previously. On this evening, Bielby was preoccupied with a mineral train, and on hearing the Signal Lad call out "Right, for the Whitby engine" with no previous instruction, presumed everything was fine and a glance at the levers mistakenly led him to believe they were correctly set, and gave permission for the boy to give the Whitby engine the signal to go – not realising anything was wrong until he heard the noise of the collision. Bielby admitted in the inquiry that he had no authority to let Signal Lad Smith work the levers, and mentioned that owing to the war, the length of night shifts had increased to eleven hours instead of the previous eight.

With the Driver Smith receiving permission to proceed, he moved to the train, and it was a dark night and there were no lights on the train as the guard had removed them, there was no way blame could be apportioned to him. Technically, the Signal Lad Smith was at fault for the crash but Signalman Bielby was the one that should have controlled the levers, or even checked properly despite breaking the rules by letting the Signal Lad move the levers. Despite this, the North Eastern Railway said Bielby was of good character. The board of enquiry found that there was no fixed signal to control running through the connection of the middle line, where the carriages were, and the excursion line where the locomotive should have ran around, and recommended one should be put in place, however the North Eastern Railway mentioned this would be difficult owing to the arrangements at the nearby Falsgrave signal box.

The next day another accident was to occur, on North Eastern metals at Chaloner Whin Junction south of York at 9.54 p.m. on 18

March, but involving a Midland Railway locomotive, 2–4–0 tender locomotive 112, operating a Midland Railway service from York to Sheffield using four North Eastern Railway carriages. With snow on the ground, the train ran over points which were in the 'intermediate' position, *i.e.* set for neither of the two lines they served, derailing the entire train at a speed of 25 mph, severely damaging the locomotive and slightly damaging the carriages. When the train was accepted on to the line, the points were set for a train heading to Doncaster, so as soon as that train passed they needed to be set for the line to Sheffield. When the Relief Signalman Timothy Self went to move the points he found they were stuck, and so sent the platelayers out to try and clean the points, presuming they or the mechanism were fouled by snow. As the platelayers were at work they saw the express bearing down upon them and got out of the way just in time. The driver of the train, Thompson Clarke, claimed that the signals were clear along with his fireman. However, Relief Signalman Self argued that they were all at danger, and when Clarke went to the signal box after the derailment to confront Self, Self pointed out that they were set at danger. Although Clarke said he could not see the signal lights as they were blocked with snow, if he looked at the rear of the signals as he passed them he would see they were at red – although even this claim was disputed as others, including the Chargeman of the platelayers, said that the lights could be seen from a reasonable distance. The crash was deemed to be caused by the driver passing signals at danger – even if he could not see the signal light he claimed was blocked with snow, he should have therefore treated it as 'at danger' and taken steps to stop the train as soon as possible, which he didn't, backed up by those who witnessed the speed of the train prior to the derailment and the Midland Railway guard of the train who noticed no difference in speed until it left the rails.

Despite this, the Relief Signalman had broken Block Rule 4 (d) which stated that after a train had been accepted on to a section, no obstruction to that train in the section could be allowed, and having the points in the 'intermediate' position, even if briefly, constituted an obstruction. The North Eastern Railway argued against this, stating that busy junctions such as Chaloner Whin could not operate without breaking this rule, and took responsibility for this. Signals passed at danger was a frequent cause of accidents, and at the time the North Eastern Railway had installed apparatus to guard against this elsewhere, but not at Chaloner Whin. At any rate the apparatus was only fitted to North Eastern Railway locomotives so even if it had been fitted at Chaloner Whin it would not have avoided the accident happening to a Midland Railway or other company's train which also used the junction.

Eric C. Geddes

March 1915 saw a failed offensive in France at the Battle of Neuve Chapelle, fought between 10–13 March, and although the preliminary thirty-five minute bombardment before the soldiers went over the top saw more shells fired than during the entire Second Boer War, there was still not nearly enough shells as needed for both the opening bombardment and ensuing battle, and was the major contributing factor to the failure of the offensive. The small amount of shells being produced, being in no way sufficient for the war to carry on at the level it was, never mind to cope with the rapid expansion of the armed forces at that time, came under intense criticism and became known as the 'Shell Scandal', leading to the creation of the Ministry of Munitions in May 1915. Eric Campbell Geddes, Deputy General Manager of the North Eastern Railway, was chosen to be the Deputy Director General of Munitions Supply upon its creation, and following his excellent services rendered he was included in the list of 'Birthday Honours' for Knighthood on 3 June 1916. During the Battle of the Somme it became all too readily apparent that the British Army did not have the mobility needed to undertake large operations on the western front, and so Geddes was sent to France to report on the situation. He recommended that better use be made of standard gauge railways for logistics, which would lead to the large expansion of the Railway Operating Division of the Royal Engineers in 1917, which included 2,000 miles of track laid down on the western front and many locomotives being shipped from British railways to France and other theatres the British Army was fighting in, such as Salonika. In October 1916 he was made Director General of Military Railways and also Inspector General of Transportation as Honorary Major General (as he was still a civilian), and had a special eight carriage train made for him for use as a travelling office by the North Eastern Railway at York. He was recalled to England in May 1917 and became First Lord of the Admiralty in July 1917 as part of Prime Minister Lloyd George's Cabinet – despite his lack of knowledge of naval operations which made his appointment to the role very surprising to many, not least political commentators. However his expertise in logistics and supply was what brought him into the role, and he worked hard to ensure shipbuilding levels were increased to counter the heavy losses of unrestricted submarine warfare being undertaken by the German U-boats. In January 1919 Geddes was knighted and in the same month he left the Admiralty, being asked by Lloyd George to become the Minister of Transport when this new Ministry was set up, a role which he undertook in August 1919 until 1921.

First air raid

Attacked from the sea for the first time in December the year previously, the north-east of England was attacked from the air for the first time on the night of 14–15 April when Imperial German Navy Zeppelin L9 flew over the coast from Blyth to South Shields, seemingly indiscriminately dropping bombs, most of which landed in fields. Two people were injured, and a photo was printed in the *North Eastern Railway Magazine* of a badly damaged bed in a house in Wallsend, presumably hit by an incendiary bomb, which a few minutes later would have had an infant sleeping in, as its mother was bathing it when the bomb struck.

Munitions Factories

In early 1915, a new building was erected by the Darlington North Road Works, which would become known as the Darlington National Projectile Factory, also known as the 'Shell Shop'. It was one of many munitions factories built in Britain, most of which were built in 1915 following the formation of the Ministry of Munitions. The story of the 'Shell Shop' is told in another chapter, but elsewhere along the network other munitions factories were either extended or built, including that at Barnbow, Leeds, where an H Class locomotive was sent to work. A correspondent to the *North Eastern Railway Magazine* described the construction of the Barnbow factory, which was officially known as National Filling Factory No. 1 – unlike the Darlington 'Shell Shop' which just produced the metal shells and brass cases *etc*, at Barnbow the shells were filled with explosives, which was much more dangerous. Rumours abounded when materials started to arrive at the site of the Barnbow factory, and along with it representatives of a large London-based building contractors, and shortly the erection of 'the outline of four vast sheds'. Despite the previous rumours that there was to be a shell factory built in the area, another rumour then started from 'some local wiseacres' that it was to be an aerodrome, however, as one North Eastern Railway staff member working at the goods station nearby put it:

We were learned enough in aviation to inform them that such places are not generally built on the banks of a wide river. The latter is not an ideal landing place for aircraft.

The correspondent continues:

Other enterprising people thought that destitute Belgians were to be housed. The only definite information we could elicit was that the sheds were in some way connected with shells. This word "shells" which was rarely used in everyday conversation before the present struggle of nations, seems now to be one of the most commonly used words in the English vocabulary.

To accompany the large buildings, a railway siding was also constructed by Canadian Pioneers, the completion of which was shortly followed by 40 to 50 wagons a day arriving for unloading only, again by the Canadian Pioneers and assisted by members of the Volunteer Training Corps in the evening. Once completed, the factory was mainly staffed by women munitions workers, who would also become known as 'munitionettes'. The Barnbow munitionettes and others who worked with TNT acquired another nickname – 'canary girls', coming from the very unfortunate side product of handling toxic TNT which turned skin a yellow colour. Although other chemicals used in munitions factories could be harmful to health and prove fatal, including the 'dope' used to varnish and tighten the linen used in the construction of aircraft fuselages and wings, TNT was by far the leading cause of most health problems and deaths amongst munitions workers. The TNT caused jaundice, made hair turn bright ginger (or sometimes even green), and even caused items touched by those affected by TNT poisoning to turn yellow – in munitions factory canteens TNT workers would have their own area as the chairs and tables would be turned yellow. It would not be until mid-1916 when the dangers caused by TNT poisoning were dealt with, by improving ventilation and conditions for workers dealing with TNT as well as other measures, which did have an effect on the mortality rate amongst munitions workers, but jaundice was still occurring and women and men were still dying. As well as the dangers of continued exposure to TNT, the danger of explosion was also a very real one, and three occurred at Barnbow, the first on 5 December 1916. Shortly after a new shift started at 10.07 p.m., whilst 4.5 inch howitzer shells were being filled, fused and packed ready for shipment to the front, in Room 42 where loaded shells would have the fuse added and screwed down into the nose of the shell, an explosion immediately killed thirty five women out of about 170 working in the room at the time, with many more being horrifically injured, the uninjured immediately going to the aid of the wounded. This only briefly interrupted production – after what remained of the bodies were removed (many were only identified from their identity discs), women from elsewhere in the factory volunteered to work in Room 42 and the work continued. Two female munitions workers were killed in another explosion in April 1917, and three men were killed in May 1918.

North Eastern Railway men saving lives

Two life-saving events by a member of serving North Eastern Railway staff occurred within months of each other in 1915 – the first was that by Henry Charles, a clerk in the General Manager's Office at York who was on holiday in Exeter in Easter 1915 when he rescued a young lady from drowning. Charles jumped into deep water and the young lady he was trying to rescue clutched him immediately and in her panic almost drowned the both of them, pulling him under water twice before able to gain the bank of the water and helped out by people on shore. The feat is made more impressive by the fact that Charles, aged just eighteen, had only learnt to swim nine months previously. By 1916 Charles was a private in the 2/6th Northumberland Fusiliers, and after church parade one Sunday was called out of the ranks in front of his entire battalion (of around 800-1,000 men) to be handed a parchment certificate from the Royal Humane Society by the Colonel of his battalion for his life saving deed.

The other life-saving event was rewarded on 12 July 1915 when Mr D. Humphreys, a porter at Murton station, was at Buckingham Palace where King George V pinned on Humphreys' breast the King Edward Medal, 2nd Class for his heroic actions. The date of the incident is not recorded, but the action happened when a young lady standing on the platform fell on to the railway line as a train was entering the station. The young lady had difficulty in getting herself up with the train rapidly approaching when Humphreys, with selfless regard, dived in front of the train, and without time to get clear, held her between the rails as the train passed over them until it could be stopped and they could both be retrieved. The driver of the train's engine said it was only five yards away from hitting the young lady when Humphreys jumped down to save her. The *North Eastern Railway Magazine* reported that "It would be difficult even to invent an instance better illustrating the exercise of two of the grandest attributes a man can possess – courage and the capacity for quick and effective action in an emergency". Humphreys, a young man, had previously stated at another presentation where he was awarded for his actions that he would be fighting for his country but for the state of his health which precluded him from doing so (the awards totalled the King Edward Medal, a silver watch and sum of £15 from the Carnegie Heroes Fund, a £20 purse of gold from the public of Murton and North Eastern Railway staff, and a further £10 from the Murton Miners' Union). Unfortunately after receiving his King Edward Medal he had been compelled to enter a sanatorium as his illness had worsened. It is not mentioned what he was suffering from, but in the early twentieth century large numbers of people suffered from tuberculosis, known at the time as consumption, which was Britain's biggest health problem at the start of the century, with large numbers of sanatoriums set up to deal with the problem. Sadly it was reported in late 1915 that Humphreys had died.

Health and safety on the railways

The relative lack of health and safety for workers resulted in many deaths and injuries on the railways during this era – and in mid-1915 instructive articles regarding safety were circulated to staff in an illustrated booklet entitled "The Safety Movement". This initiative was started by the Great Western Railway, and the opening paragraph is particularly thought provoking on the risks taken by men which could lead to injuries or even loss of life, especially considering accidents during the war period that occurred on the North Eastern Railway:

> Human lives are cheap. Dirt Cheap. Men risk them for nothing. They sell them like old crocks. They do, really. Men will take their lives in their hands to save a few yards' walk, or to save waiting a minute or two. They'll even do it for fun.

Another worker lost his life on the North Eastern Railway on 29 October at Hull Paragon station. The foreman porter, 64 year old J. E. Cocker, was despatching the 8.05 p.m. train to Selby on a foggy night. He walked along the platform to see if he could find the locomotive for the train on its way to the station from the engine shed, and when he saw it approaching he was guiding it with his hand lamp when he fell from the station platform on to the railway line, and the locomotive ran him over, killing him. J. E. Cocker had been in the employ of the North Eastern Railway since 1874, originally at Hull goods station, and transferred to the passenger department in 1903.

Roll of Honour

The roll of honour of North Eastern Railway men killed in the service of their King and Country made up a large part of the *North Eastern Railway Magazine* during the war. Sadly it was the focus of criticism by at least one reader in the summer of 1915, leading to this reply published in the August 1915 edition of the magazine:

> We have received one or two expressions of opinion that too large an amount of our space is being devoted to matters relating to the

war. To our mind such criticisms do not seem altogether generous. We believe that the Magazine is fulfilling its legitimate purpose as a publication for the whole of the staff in recording items of interest about those of our number who have so bravely responded to their country's call.

It is only fitting, we think, to collect for our Roll of Honour details of the men who have fallen while doing their duty; while no less worthy of a place in our pages are the letters from those NER men who remain undismayed and even cheerful amid danger almost inconceivable to us at home. Some of the communications one can scarcely read with undimmed eyes.

We like to think that in the bound volumes of this magazine there will be preserved for future generations a more or less adequate record of the great part played by NER men of every grade in this time of national crisis.

Raven to Woolwich

The Locomotive Department of the North Eastern Railway lost its Chief Mechanical Engineer on 15 September 1915, when Vincent Litchfield Raven went to Woolwich Arsenal to run the vast munitions works there, producing both the shells and the guns that fired them. Raven was requested by the Minister of Munitions himself, David Lloyd George, who was to become Prime Minister on 6 December 1916. It is likely that Raven had been recommended by Eric Geddes, and also that Raven's loss would not be too hard hitting owing to the effectiveness of his deputy, Arthur Cowie Stamer, who was more than capable of taking up the reins. Raven took up the post of Acting Chief Superintendent of Ordnance Factories at Woolwich (the original Chief Superintendent, Sir Frederick Donaldson had been sent to work in Canada and the USA to organise supplies to be brought from there) and immediately went to work in improving the output and efficiency there. Within a few months it was announced by Lloyd George in the House of Commons on 20 December that since Raven's appointment, there had been a 60-80 per cent increase in production with just a 23 per cent increase in workforce. One of Raven's influences at the Arsenal was his work on the internal railway – no mean task as there were over 150 miles of railway on the site, and not in the same gauge either. To cope with the increase in production and also as part of Raven's work to standardise the railways at the Arsenal, in November 1915 four North Eastern Railway locomotives were hired to work on the Royal Arsenal Railway. It is likely these were hired owing to Raven's influence, and also that owing to the reduction in activity at docks on the North Eastern Railway system, them possibly being out of use at the time. The four locomotives were all 0-4-0T's, one K Class number 559 of 1890, and three H Class locomotives, numbers 129, 587 and 898, built in 1888. All four returned to the NER, 898 not returning until January 1919. Along with four North Eastern Railway locomotives, fifty wagons were hired from the NER at a set rate of 6 shillings per week (later reduced to 5 shillings) to cope with increased demand on the Royal Arsenal Railway. Raven was knighted in 1917 for his work at Woolwich Arsenal, and continued to work there until the war was over – however he still kept in touch with the North Eastern Railway, and made visits back to the railway whenever possible.

Accident at Crakehall

On 24 September station master George Potter of Crakehall station on the Wensleydale Branch died from injuries after falling between a moving train and the platform. He had just signalled a passenger train away but then hurried towards one of the rear carriages, possibly believing that one of the doors was not secured. As he ran towards the moving train, he collided with a member of staff walking in the opposite direction, and he then fell between the train and platform. Despite being rushed to Rutson Hospital in Northallerton, he died from his injuries. Potter was sixty-four, and had been in North Eastern Railway service since May 1873.

Refreshments for servicemen

With the large amount of troop movements by rail, canteens and buffets were being set up at large stations all over the country, often by the YMCA, to provide refreshments for weary troops, and York was no exception. A committee of York ladies approached the North Eastern Railway with regards to the idea of forming a buffet of light refreshments at low charges to soldiers and sailors in uniform, to be kept open night and day by volunteers. The North Eastern Railway agreed to provide an area for the ladies to run the canteen, and also provided two converted vehicles for use – a saloon carriage used as a buffet, and a van with a kitchen installed and a retiring room for the volunteers, both vehicles being fitted with gas fires for comfort. The buffet vehicles were placed in a platform facing the main south platform for troops heading towards the continent, but wheeled trolleys meant a mobile service could take place to serve other parts of the station. The buffet was opened on 15 November by Major H. A. Watson, who commented on the buffet's 'obvious advantages, and said he hoped the station staff would direct to it any member of His Majesty's forces who might be waiting for trains and who looked as though they could do with some refreshment'. A year-and-a-half after it opened it was reported in the April 1917 edition of the *North Eastern Railway Magazine* that 'one only has to enter the station at any hour of the day or night to realise how great a work the ladies who run the buffet are doing.' By 1917 the staff of the buffet consisted of a president, four caterers, three secretaries, a treasurer, forty-five managers and around two hundred and sixty helpers. Mugs and other ancillary items, not including food, averaged around £12 a week, and on average 18,000 men a week were served by the buffet service. It was recorded that in the first twelve months of the buffet since opening, £7,630 was spent on food, tea, coffee *etc.*, and in the fourteen months since it opened, 898,500 men had been served. One North Eastern Railway member of staff who sometimes had to make night journeys, commented in late 1918 how busy York was at night time, "but what struck him most was the unselfish service given by the ladies at the soldiers' and sailors' canteen, where business was very brisk indeed".

Changes to the workforce

By the start of 1915 women were starting to be employed by the North Eastern Railway itself to cope with manpower shortages – the first evidence of this being a photograph of three women porters at

Leeds New station, in specially-made women's uniforms. The role of women was to become more and more important to the North Eastern Railway as the war went on, and a comprehensive chapter on the subject is dedicated to them.

Ambulance man saves a life

On 2 October, Mr J. Willis was given a special certificate for ambulance men, following his services rendered when a miner fell between a train and the platform at Hesleden station. The train was moving at the time and the wheels of a carriage passed over his left arm, and the man also suffered severe cuts, bruises and a broken clavicle. The doctor who arrived on the scene and tended to the miner before he was sent to hospital said that Willis's actions immediately after the man fell without doubt saved his life.

Micklefield collision

The snow was falling heavily on the night of 9 December 1915 when the 6.15 p.m. Up York to Leeds passenger train, hauled by R Class 4-4-0 1217 driven by T. Gregory neared Micklefield. Driver Gregory was struggling to see the signals, and stepped over to the left side of the cab to try and see the signal as the engine lurched and he was thrown across the cab. He had already turned off steam as he knew he was near a signal and the train was travelling between eight and ten miles per hour. By the time he got up and applied the brakes the engine had already left the line as it went over points set for the 6.30 p.m. Down Leeds to Hull service. The derailed train had only stopped for a moment or so when it was hit by M Class 4-4-0 1622 hauling the Leeds to Hull passenger service driven by T. Proctor, who was braking as the signals were at danger but as the engine slowed down, he could see the sparks coming from the braking of the engine ahead, shortly before the two locomotives collided. The locomotives hit right buffer to right buffer, so both were pushed outwards by the force of the collision, the moving Leeds to Hull service being brought to a stop by the mound of the earth which was at the end of an adjoining siding.

Driver Gregory of the York to Leeds service recalled the oncoming locomotive seemingly slide along the footplate of his stationary engine, until he was knocked out as the leading carriage hit him on the head. There were nine injuries in total – six passengers suffered light injuries, and the driver and fireman of the York to Leeds service were injured, as was the driver of the Leeds to Hull. The enquiry found that Driver Gregory of the York to Leeds service was at fault for the crash, as before the signal at danger which he had noticed, he had already passed a signal at danger further back along the line. Both he and the Fireman, F. Pringle, claimed that it was at clear, but with the arrangement of the track work this could not have been possible – the only possible explanation being that the weight of snow pushed the semaphore signal arms down and shown a green light instead of red, but if this was the case, which would be extraordinary, then it would surely have happened to other signals in the vicinity, but none were. The damage to the locomotives included bent bogie frames and main frames to R Class 1217, as well as the buffer beam and buffers broken which received the brunt of the impact, and M Class 1622 also had its bogie frames bent and distorted, with the right leading bogie wheel completely shorn off.

Disaster at St Bede's Junction

A series of errors caused a horrific crash at St Bede's Junction near Jarrow on the dark, foggy morning of 17 December 1915 at 7.20 a.m. that would leave nineteen dead and eighty one injured, in a crash that echoed Gretna Green earlier that year. St Bede's Junction was on the main line between South Shields and Newcastle, consisting of two parallel lines on an embankment around twenty feet high, the lines running almost precisely east/west, the Up line to Newcastle being on the southern side, and the Down line to South Shields on the northern side, with a branch heading down to Tyne Dock Bottom.

The 6.50 a.m. goods train from Tyne Dock Bottom was being assisted at the rear by E1 Class 0-6-0T tank engine 2182 that morning, driven by William Hunter with eighteen-year-old Acting Fireman Robert Jewett. The banking of goods trains from Tyne Dock had become fairly commonplace, however was never officially authorised by the North Eastern Railway, and as such there was no authorised signal between the signal boxes controlling the Tyne Dock Bottom Branch to let each other know that there is an engine assisting, which would leave the train at St Bede's Junction and require a clear path to return to Tyne Dock. To do this, the engine would stop in a position where it could be seen from the signal box at St Bede's Junction, and if not seen then Rule 55 would apply, which meant that if the train was left standing for three minutes in clear weather, or immediately in the dark or other conditions which would affect visibility such as rain or fog, then the fireman, guard or other member of staff connected with the train or locomotive would go to the signal box to inform the signalman of their presence and intentions.

Locomotive 2182 stopped at St Bede's Junction, and the goods train continued – 2182 was not coupled to the goods train so that it did not require stopping at the top, and already had a green light on the bunker at the rear and a red light at the front, so although this would not be correct for when it was travelling forward, *i.e.* as it was when banking the goods train, it was all set for the return journey. The locomotive came to a stop at 6.55, reversed back slightly to be able to see the signal boards, and waited. A Down goods passed them going to Tyne Dock, and after that the signal to Tyne Dock went to danger. Driver Hunter whistled to make the signalman aware of his presence but it stayed at danger, and the signal for the Down main line was lowered. Hunter explained Rule 55 to Jewett, who was not aware of the rule and had not had to observe it before, and said he should go to the signal box if they were not let away after the next Down main line service passed. After it passed, they were still not let away so Jewett was given a hand lamp and proceeded to the signal box at 7.13. By then, Signalman William Hodgson, not aware of the presence of the light engine, had accepted the Up 7.05 a.m. passenger service from South Shields to Newcastle, although he had not received the 'out of section' message from Jarrow regarding the Down goods until 7.11. He had not realised there was an engine assisting the 6.50 a.m. goods as he could not see it nor any of the lights on it, and as the brake van of the goods had side lights, this generally meant that there was not an assisting engine, although not a hard and fast rule. At 7.12 a.m. the signalman also accepted the Down empty from Hebburn to South Shields. As Fireman Jewett neared the signal box, in the distance he could hear a train. When he reached the signal box at 7.14, the signalman came out and after being told of the presence of the light engine said he was not aware of it being there, and immediately told him to put his hand lamp on red and show it to the coming Up passenger service and then changed all signals to danger. Driver William James Smith of the Up service, despite the thick fog meaning he could only see the signals when he was about an engine's length away from them, saw the signals as clear when he passed them. Driver Smith thought he saw the trailing edge of the tender of another locomotive in front, but as it was only a short distance in front there was no time to do anything, and despite shutting off steam and applying brakes he was not sure if this happened before the crash or just as it happened. The first his other crew member, Fireman Frank McArdle, knew of the light engine was when he heard a noise as they struck the other locomotive. In the seconds leading up to the crash, Driver Hunter had heard the rumbling of an oncoming train, and realising it was on the same line, then seeing the head lamps oncoming, blew his whistle as a warning and tried to move the locomotive forward to lessen the impact speed, but only got to around four or five miles per hour when the Up passenger train, the 7.05 a.m. South Shields to Newcastle service, consisting of five carriages led by O Class 0-4-4T 1867, ran into the back of 2182 at a speed of around 30 mph, sending 2182 to the right across the Down line, and 1867 of the Up train going right and falling down the embankment. The force of the collision broke the coupling between the locomotive and the carriages, but the second carriage was forced into the leading carriage, telescoping them together and completely smashing the rearmost three compartments of the leading carriage. Shortly after, the 6.58 a.m. Down empty passenger train consisting of six carriages hauled by A Class 2-4-2T 671 running at the speed of approximately 10 mph, ran into the light engine which was now fouling the Down line, forcing the engine of the Down empty 671 to its right down the embankment, and 2182 almost completely reversing itself, being thrown back onto the other side of the Up line and now lying on its side down the embankment along with the engine of the Up passenger service. The fireman of the Down empty was killed, and the driver lost consciousness, and when he regained it he was lying on the embankment near the engine. Driver Hunter of the light engine did not remember anything after the engine left the rails, the next thing he realised was that he standing in a field at the bottom of the embankment.

Fireman Jewett immediately headed towards the scene of the crash, but Guard Alexander Mitchell of the Up train met him on the way and gave him fog signals (detonators to be placed on the tracks to explode when ran over by a train, the loud noise telling the driver to stop as soon as possible) to protect the Up line. By the time he had done this and returned to the site of the crash, two of the carriages were on fire.

Immediately after the crash, Driver Samson Tolliday leapt into action – Tolliday was off duty but was riding in the second carriage of the Up train to Newcastle, having got on board at Tyne Dock and having to go in the second carriage as the first carriage was so full, a decision which probably saved his life. As the carriage he was in derailed, the other four passengers in his carriage started to panic, but he told them to keep cool, but upon the carriage stopping found that it was so damaged he could not open the door. Lowering the window he slid out, falling on to the embankment below, and encouraged his fellow passengers to follow suit, which they did. Tolliday was a member of the North Eastern Railway ambulance, the first railway in the country to have an ambulance which certainly paid off in cases of accidents and other emergencies such as the East Coast bombardment almost exactly a year previously. Seeing other passengers trapped in carriages, he sent men to get the tools from the rescue boxes which he knew the North Eastern Railway had fitted to most of the brake carriages for use in emergencies such as this, containing crowbars, a saw, hammer, fire buckets, hand lamps, folding ladders *etc*. Tolliday was in the second compartment from the leading edge of his carriage, and could see men trapped in the leading compartment. He managed to get three out, but saw others trapped as the compartment had collapsed upon them, so when the other passengers he had previously sent to get tools returned, he set to retrieving the trapped men. He was getting a fourth person out of the wreckage when fire broke out from the gas cylinder located directly underneath the compartment, the gas being used to light the carriages but had been responsible for devastating fires with loss of life, the most horrifying being the Gretna Green disaster, the biggest loss of life on Britain's railways. Tolliday saw the small jet of flame rise from the cylinder and immediately sent three men to get fire extinguishers, also carried in the brake carriages. He had to leave the trapped men and went underneath the carriage to try and put the fire out in the vicinity of the cylinder directly, but although extremely proficient with a fire extinguisher from the ambulance classes had no luck in putting it out. Getting a second extinguisher he went to the side of the carriage the passengers were trapped in to try and extinguish it from there, again unable to do so. The flames were now rising and were spreading to the top of the carriage, threatening to burn the trapped passengers alive. Tolliday now stood on top of the carriage directing the extinguisher to the fire there in an attempt to rescue them, and although again it did not work he stayed until the roof started to give away and his face was burnt. With the roof collapsing, he got off and tried to get the passengers out with the assistance of Driver Rowe who was on duty at St Bede's Sidings prior to the crash, and managed to get one man out who was severely burnt with a broken leg. By now the flames had engulfed the carriage and the heat had become too much and he had to leave the two men trapped inside. He went and searched the other compartments of the train but saw only dead bodies, he thought he saw one person escape the train after the collision and did not hear any cries for help since then, to him the bodies seemed to have been killed in the initial collision. One of the men Tolliday helped to escape could have been Bill Watson, a carpenter at the Jarrow Munitions Factory, who with his workmates was trapped in a compartment of the second carriage.

Not all of those assisting were survivors of the crash – around a dozen local women who were aware of the crash went to help, who crawled through the wreckage to look for survivors whilst others ran to the doctors, and others back to their homes to fetch blankets and hot water bottles. One of those that stayed was a Mrs Betty Flanagan, who crept under one of the burning carriages and pulled two men to safety, although she was badly burned herself. Despite the attempts of Tolliday and others, the leading carriage of the Up train was completely consumed by the flames, and the leading end of second carriage was too. The leading carriage of the Down empty ended up close to the telescoped leading and second carriages of the Up train and was also consumed by the flames, leaving just a part of the compartment at the end of the carriage untouched. The fire burnt until the fire brigade arrived an hour after the crash occurred. At around 10.10 a Doctor told Tolliday to go home, which he did.

The enquiry found that three separate causes attributed to the crash. The first was that there was no code signal used to notify the signalman at St Bede's Junction that there was a pilot engine assisting a train coming up from Tyne Dock Bottom. The signalmen at either boxes could not be held at fault for this, as there was no signal code that could be applied to this situation authorised by use on the branch by the North Eastern Railway. The reply from the North Eastern Railway was that there was no code authorised because the use of an engine to assist trains from Tyne Dock Bottom was not authorised, even though it had been happening frequently in recent years.

The second attributing factor to the collision was down to the fault of Signalman Hodgson at St Bede's Junction – although there was no code for assisting engines, he admitted that engines frequently assisted trains up to St Bede's Junction and then required routing back to Tyne Dock Bottom, so he should have kept a special lookout for an assisting engine and assumed that there was one, instead of assuming there wasn't one, especially on such a dark and foggy morning with severely reduced visibility.

Thirdly, another factor which lead to the collision was the delay in Acting Fireman Jewett of the assisting engine, 2182, in going to the St Bede's Junction signal box, as per Rule 55. As mentioned previously, the engine came to a standstill at 6.55 but the fireman did not leave the engine until 7.12, reaching the signal box at 7.13, leaving little time for the signalman to act before the collision. The seventeen minute delay was found to be unacceptable, and Driver Hunter's excuses in keeping Jewett on the engine which were firstly that the signalman would have been preoccupied with the Down traffic which he noticed the clear path for when they came to a standstill, and after that passed, the second excuse that Jewett would be in danger of being ran over by another train if he left the engine were found to be invalid, especially the excuse of Jewett being in danger as the route to the signal box would not have taken him over any of the lines in use at the time. Although as the driver he was in a senior position of authority on the engine, and Jewett was relatively fresh, having been a fireman for seven months previously, Jewett was not completely without blame as he had still been with the company for three and a half years, and should have been well acquainted with the rule book and Rule 55 especially, and should have taken some responsibility instead of simply acting on the driver's instructions throughout.

It was not found possible to exactly determine the source of the subsequent fire which resulted in two or three further deaths, however off duty Driver Tolliday's description of seeing a rising flame from the gas cylinder immediately underneath the leading compartment of the second carriage was accepted as accurate owing to his proximity to the fire when it broke out. Several gas cylinders of carriages involved in the collision were found afterwards to have burst ends, which was believed to have happened upon collision and the gas escaping then, which is perhaps fortunate as it may have added to the conflagration when the subsequent fire started and spread. Following the fire, identification of the bodies in the leading and second carriages of the Up passenger service was very difficult. However, it was believed they had all been killed in the initial collision, baring one or two in the second carriage who it was believed, and was backed up by Tolliday's recounting of trying to rescue two men in the second carriage, who were killed by the fire, a horrific way to die, which must have been extremely distressing for Tolliday and others who had tried so valiantly to try and get them out of the wreckage.

The enquiry focused on the dangers of gas-lit vehicles and mentioned previous cases where gas lighting had led to fires which had increased the death toll in railway crashes – Hawes Junction in 1910, Ditton in 1912, and of course Gretna Green earlier that year. A. C. Stamer, the Acting Chief Mechanical Engineer of the North Eastern Railway, stressed that the North Eastern Railway was well aware of the danger of fires after a railway accident, and was taking measures to prevent these where possible – he mentioned that the entire Tyneside electric rolling stock of 1904 was fitted with electric lighting, and that in the past three years all newly-built carriages were fitted with electric lighting, and although plans were underway to convert gas-lit carriages to electric, the war had forced these plans to be shelved, producing a figure recorded on 31 December 1914 that out of 4,241 carriages owned by the North Eastern Railway at the time, 626 of those had electric lighting. At the same time, new carriages were being built with non-flammable material that would not catch light as easily, but again conversion of older carriages had to be put on hold for the duration of the war, although as of early 1916 344 carriages had been fitted with new materials. As a further measure, 770 brake carriages and vans had been fitted with rescue appliances and fire extinguishers out of 836 in total, and these tools and extinguishers had been used to good effect in the St Bede's Junction crash, notably in saving as many as possible from the wrecked second carriage before the fire started and eventually consumed the carriage. Furthermore, 924 vehicles were fitted with a lead pipe on the gas regulator, which, if hit by a hammer following a crash, would close the gas supply hopefully preventing a fire. The use of flat buffers on rolling stock was also being introduced to replace convex buffers to reduce the risk of one carriage overriding another one and causing the horrific 'telescoping' effect which resulted in the main loss of life in this instance. Since the crash, by February 1916 the North Eastern Railway had added more straps to the gas cylinders underneath carriages to house them more securely, which would hopefully prevent them from breaking loose in an accident. Incandescent lighting had been fitted to 334 carriages, reducing the amount of gas cylinders that needed to be carried down to just one, from in some cases three or four.

Eight members of staff received marks of appreciation of conduct by Directors of the North Eastern Railway on 11 May 1916, at a meeting presided by A. C. Stamer. Salmson Tolliday was especially commended, by Sir Walter Plummer on behalf of the North Eastern Railway directors. He was presented with a gold watch and chain, as well as an ambulance medallion for meritorious conduct. Fireman D. Cresswell received a silver watch and chain and medallion. Medallions were also presented to Foreman David Scott, Driver W. Rowe who had been on duty at St Bede's Junction, Fitter J. Allison of Tyne Dock, A. Thompson, blacksmith at Tyne Dock, A. Thompson Junior, joiner at Tyne Dock, and J. C. Hindmarsh, joiner at Park Lane Gateshead.

Landslip

Heavy rainfall at the end of the year created unpleasant condition on the western front, especially in the Ypres area where the water table was, and still is, very high at any time of year meaning an uncomfortable Christmas for those in the trenches. On the North Eastern Railway, the rainfall caused at least one landslip, occurring on the Tyneside electrified railway a quarter of a mile west of St Anthony's station, where the railway line is on an embankment alongside the River Tyne – the rains caused a length of track around 100 feet long to dangle in the air, disrupting services in the area until repaired.

The Shildon to Newport
Electrification

The electrification of tramways in the UK during the late nineteenth and early twentieth centuries resulted in a loss of passengers for suburban passenger services in those areas – the electric trams were cheaper and faster than the horse-drawn predecessors making them a more attractive alternative to the railways. The North Eastern Railway was no exception to this, and when the Newcastle Corporation Tramways started electric services in December 1901, the rapid rise in passenger figures it brought accompanied a fall in passenger figures for the North Eastern Railway, and the decision was made to electrify thirty-seven miles of suburban railways in the Tyneside area, focused on Newcastle Central and reaching out to Tynemouth and Whitley Bay before heading back to Newcastle Central. The electric powered carriages, which would become known as Electric Multiple Units, were powered using a third electrified rail mounted to the side of the railway line, and the current collected from a 'shoe' fitted on the bogie of the powered units. The carriages and motor cars for the line were built in 1903 and the electrified route opened in stages during 1904, and was a great success, improving the popularity of the electric services. At the same time, two electric locomotives were built to operate on the short but lucrative Newcastle Quayside Branch, which operated from Trafalgar Yard near Manors Station, down a steep semi-circular branch mostly in tunnels to the quayside below, where steam locomotives would shunt the wagons. Steam locomotives had previously been used in the tunnels but there were problems with the sparks from the locomotives setting light to the straw used to pack goods in the open wagons behind, and also there were visibility problems due to the steam. Like the suburban services, the electric locomotives which were introduced into service in June 1905 following trials were a great success, and were not replaced until 1964. Unlike the third rail only Tyneside services, the Quayside electric locomotives used a mix of third rail and overhead catenary wires, the current being collected by a pantograph fitted on the cab roof (the locomotives originally had a bow collector fitted on one of the sloping bonnets at either end of the locomotive, but this was found unsatisfactory following trials and both locomotives had the cab roof pantograph by the time they entered service), the catenary wires being used at either ends of the tunnel at Trafalgar Yard and the Quayside. The third rail being used in the tunnels where clearance was restricted (which required the pantograph to be brought down before entering the tunnel mouth and raised on exiting) and also to transit back to the Tyneside electric car sheds at South Gosforth where the locomotives were also stabled when not in use. The success of the electric services provoked the North Eastern Railway into considering further electrification, and Chief Mechanical Engineer Vincent Raven was one of the leading proponents of the benefits of electric traction following his heavy involvement in the Tyneside electrification whilst under CME of the time Wilson Worsdell.

A visit to the USA was funded by the company, the second for Raven as he had visited before in 1902 to see how railways were run there and bring back any ideas that could be applicable to British railways. The second visit in 1911 was to research electrification of railways there, and Raven took his deputy, A. C. Stamer, who would become the Acting Chief Mechanical Engineer during the war years following Raven's appointment to the Ministry of Munitions, and a young Edward Thompson, who would later become the CME of the London & North Eastern Railway. Also on the trip was Charles Merz, friend of Raven and electrical engineer who was also involved with the Tyneside electrification as consulting engineer. The visit spurred Raven on further, and he was quick to write a report on his return, published in January 1912 – the estimate for electrification of a large scale section of line was deemed too high by Alexander Kaye Butterworth, who suggested that any figures for electrification could be gathered from other railways and it could be determined from them whether widespread electrification would be worth it. However, Raven persevered, and it was agreed by Butterworth and the Board of

Directors that the Shildon to Newport mineral line would be electrified as a trial, the line being relatively self-contained and not containing any tunnels or difficult junctions that would increase the cost and cause difficulties in electrifying the route. The expected cost of the electrification of the route and building ten electric locomotives, which were expected to replace seventeen steam locomotives, was £60,000.

The route chosen for the trial electrification programme was decided upon owing to the fact that if it was a failure or caused problems there would not be as much damage done to services compared with electrifying a mixed passenger/goods route. Despite this, it was still a highly profitable eighteen-and-a-half mile route from Shildon where coal was collected from the west Durham coalfield (and also where the first public railway service, the Stockton & Darlington Railway, started its first steam hauled service in 1825) to Newport at Erimus Yard from where it was then distributed to the nearby docks, blast furnaces etc. The heavy mineral traffic was often hauled by powerful T, T1 and T2 Class 0-8-0 steam locomotives, so the new electric locomotives would have to be powerful enough to deal with some of the heaviest loads on the North Eastern Railway. The line to be electrified was mainly double track, running from Shildon shed and the connection to the main line, through Shildon, including Shildon West sidings, then past Middridge Junction and Middridge Sidings, then mostly double track through Simpasture Junction to Bowesfield West Junction. Following this, at Bowesfield Junction the line went from two to three lines, then Erimus Yard which was the main terminus for electric traffic, (with a single line avoiding Erimus Yard for the 'Up' mineral traffic from Old River Junction to Thornaby) with the electrified line stretching to Middle Junction sidings slightly farther east. The length of sidings to be electrified and also the amount of double lines to be electrified meant that although the route was only eighteen-and-a-half miles, around fifty miles of track was to be electrified in total. When the locomotives were not in use, they were stabled at Shildon shed, which consisted of one large building with three turntables with 'roads' arranged around the turntable for the locomotives to be stored on. The electric locomotives were arranged around Turntable Three, and half of the roads around the turntable, the turntable and the line running up to the turntable had to be fitted with overhead wires.

The route was to be fitted with overhead catenary wires throughout, and the go ahead for the electrification was given in 1913, with construction starting that year in June. The route required two electrical substations to be built, one at Erimus and the other at Aycliffe, and the overhead lines supplied electricity at 1,500 volts to the locomotives. The locomotives designed for the route were 1,100 hp Bo-Bo locomotives, the wheels arranged into two four-wheel bogies. The locomotives had two pantographs, both on the cab roof, the cab being in the centre of the locomotive with bonnets at each end. Unlike the two Quayside branch locomotives which were built by British Thomson Houston Co. Ltd, with mechanical parts sub-contracted to Brush Electrical Engineering Company of Loughborough, the Shildon locomotives were built by the North Eastern Railway at Darlington North Road Works, with the electrical parts made and fitted to the locomotives by Siemens. The locomotives were ordered in May 1913, and the first was completed by May 1914 although it would be another year until the line would be ready for them to run on. They weighed in at 74 tons with four motors, two motors powering each bogie (however they were connected so would both run the same) with an optimum haulage capacity of 1,400 tons, based on a speed of 25 mph. The work on the electrification of the line was done with minimal disruption to the mineral traffic working on the line – the overhead wires were mostly hung from a gantry which stretched across the width of the entire track bed from two vertical posts on each side of the railway line. The vertical posts were a permanent fixture, and during construction were used to raise the horizontal gantry, and then when raised into position the workmen often worked on fitting the wires whilst stood on wooden planks with steam locomotives passing directly beneath them. The overhead steel gantries were usually placed every 110 yards, but placed more closely on sidings and curves, and consisted of a double wire except where the maximum power would be not be necessary, such as sidings or where the train would be going downhill where gravity would assist with the load. Warning signs were placed along the line, warning railway staff and the public alike of the dangerous electric wires, and wood boards fitted on bridges in case those on the bridge got too close or fell off. On the locomotives themselves, the pantographs were raised and held in the raised position where they could contact the overhead wires using compressed air, with a manual hand pump as back-up in case there was not any compressed air in the reservoir when the locomotive started service, so that if air pressure was lost the pantographs would automatically lower and lose electrical contact. At the same time, the doors to access the electrical components could only be opened with the same removable key that was used for the compressed air cock, so they could only be opened when the pantograph was down, so no power could be running through the electrical gear, and the key released to be used on the doors.

Although ten locomotives were to be built in total, during the war only nine were built and entered service, numbered 3 to 11 (1 and 2 were the numbers given to the two electric locomotives used on the Newcastle Quayside Branch), with the final locomotive number 12 entering traffic in 1919. Upon their completion the first nine were stored at Darlington until sent to Shildon on 18 June 1915, and the electrified lines having power put through them on 21 June. The first section of the line from Middridge Sidings to Bowesfield West started to be run using the electric locomotives on 1 July 1915, the opening delayed by the war – not only was there a lack of manpower on the North Eastern Railway, but with Siemens being the contractor, and being a German company, a lot of their German staff returned to Germany in 1914. *The North Eastern Railway Magazine* front page article on the full opening of the route, published in the June 1916 edition, highlighted the benefits of electric traction;

> One of the main advantages of the change from steam to electric traction is that the electric locomotives take their power from a central station in which coal is burnt in the most economical way. With steam locomotives, on the other hand, the coal has to be burnt on the engine itself, where there are restrictions as to space and weight, which make it impossible to use the fuel in the most economical manner. Again, the electric locomotive with its simple and robust equipment of motors, requires less upkeep and repair than a steam locomotive, which must contain within itself the whole of the plant required to convert the energy of the coal into motive power. By virtue of these special features the electric locomotive can normally be kept running every hour throughout the twenty-four. Unlike the steam locomotive, it need not spend much of its time in the running shed; it does not need to take in either coal or water, or to have tubes swept.
>
> The change is equally beneficial from the standpoint of safety owing to the simplicity of the electric locomotive, the absence of fire and boiler, and the almost automatic ease of control, the driver is free to give

practically all his attention to looking out and to signals. This brings not only safety but more rapid working with less strain on the driver.

The line from Middridge Sidings westwards towards Shildon was opened on 30 October 1915, then east from Bowesfield West to Erimus on 22 November 1915, and the final section from Erimus to Newport East on 10 January 1916. For the first few months, the electric locomotives only ran at night time using three locomotives so that during the daytime minor work could be done to complete the electrification of the lines. During 1915 the locomotives ran 14,171 train miles (mileage where the locomotives were actually hauling a train, as the name implies) in total, 94,173 in 1916 and 117,078 in 1917, the first year of full operational service and in the last year of the war, 1918, the number decreased to 111,232. Of course, with many other engine sheds on the North Eastern Railway and around the country, female cleaners were employed at Shildon, and one photograph that exists today shows female cleaners at work on electric locomotive number 11. This photo sums up the North Eastern Railway in the First World War superbly – the modernity of electric traction, and the changing scene of women at work which, with the greater social freedom this would bring, would lead to great social change following the First World War.

Following the war, the economic downturn meant the amount of mineral trains decreased, and the electric locomotives never got the chance to be utilised to their full extent, and this was the only line on the system they could run on, there was no other use for them. Following the Grouping in 1923, when the North Eastern Railway became part of the London & North Eastern Railway, the locomotives continued to be used less and less, until the 1930s when it was decided that it was not economical to keep the locomotives in use, and ironically they were replaced by steam locomotives, and the gantries taken down. In 1935 when the locomotives were withdrawn from service they were taken to Darlington and stored in the paint shop. Nine of them were kept there until 1947 when they were moved to the South Gosforth car sheds, where the Tyneside electric multiple units were stabled, as were the two Quayside Branch electric locomotives, and in 1950 they were formally withdrawn from traffic and were scrapped. One of the locomotives, number 11, was granted a temporary reprieve in 1936 when it was decided that one of the locomotives would be converted to run on the Manchester to Sheffield line which was being electrified at the time. It was rebuilt in 1942 at Doncaster Works and had several modifications to it, including an increase of horsepower to 1,256 hp from the original 1,100 hp. Number 11, by now numbered 6498 by the London & North Eastern Railway, never worked on the Manchester to Sheffield line as the electrification was delayed due to the Second World War, and in 1947 went to South Gosforth and was stored with the other Shildon electric locomotives, but two years later, now with a new British Railways number as 26510, was sent down to work on the electrified Ilford Carriage Sidings in Essex, where it renumbered for a fourth time as Department Locomotive 100. It worked there until 1960 when the voltage was changed, stored until 1964 and then scrapped at Doncaster.

The initial success of the Shildon to Newport electrification lead to Raven being given permission to design an electric passenger locomotive in 1919, proposing an electrification of the York to Newcastle section of the east coast main line, and Raven visited the United States of America for a third time in 1920 to see the developments in electric railways there. Authorisation for Raven's design to be built was given in March 1920, the electrical components to be built by Metropolitan-Vickers and mechanical parts by the North Eastern Railway. The original proposal by Merz & McEllan in June 1919, who would be the consulting engineers again, was to electrify the line from York to Newcastle via Darlington and Aycliffe. Another line running from Northallerton on the east coast main line to join the Shildon to Newport line, to run into Newport and then extend onwards to Middlesbrough itself, with a branch leading from the Shildon to Newport line via Stockton and then join the line again, and then another line from the Shildon to Newport line running in a loop to serve the town of Stockton. Another line would leave the Shildon to Newport line running north to join the east coast main line at Ferryhill. The locomotive had a wheel arrangement of 4–6–4, the six wheels in the centre being driven, with two pantographs on the cab roof, in appearance looking like an enlarged version of the Shildon electric locomotives. The locomotive, number 13, was taken into service in 1922 and ran trials along the Shildon to Newport line, but the grouping meant that the electrification was not to happen, and the east coast main line was only electrified in the late twentieth century.

1916

January 1916 saw the last of the men on the Gallipoli peninsula evacuated. A munitions factory exploded in Faversham, Kent, on 3 March killing 106, and the Easter Rising took place in Ireland. The clash between the British and German fleets, awaited since the outbreak of war finally occurred on 31 May and 1 June at the Battle of Jutland – both sides claimed victory but it proved the dominance of the Royal Navy on the North Sea. On 1 July the 'big push' in what became known as the Battle of the Somme began with massive casualties on the first day. The battle raged until 18 November and introduced the tank to the battlefield for the first time, designed in secrecy by the British in 1915. The first German airship was shot down over Britain on the night of 2–3 September by William Leefe-Robinson, and from then on the Zeppelins' reign of terror over London came to an end as more are shot down. HMHS (HM Hospital Ship) Britannic *is sunk by a mine with the loss of only thirty souls on 21 November.*

Donovan the Dog

An interesting adventure came to an end on 8 February 1916 – that of an escaped Great Dane dog going by the name of Donovan. Donovan was on his way from a 'Midland station' to Scarborough on 27 November 1915 to join his owner who had recently moved there. Whilst Donovan was awaiting a connecting train at York, a porter in charge of his care tied him to a hot water pipe in the Parcels Office. This became rather uncomfortable for Donovan who managed to escape with the chain, muzzle and label and promptly disappeared. A reward for £40 was given for his capture, with advertisements placed in local newspapers and descriptions and inquiries sent to police forces in the local area for miles around. Despite this, Donovan evaded capture, scavenging for food and sleeping rough. He was mostly seen in the Fulford district of York where he becoming quite a menace as, according to one description, he had 'become wild and somewhat savage' and it 'was said he would never be taken alive'. After two months of Donovan running wild and having become both a nuisance to locals and an embarrassment to the North Eastern Railway and local police force, it was suggested that the lady owner be brought to York on the chance the two should meet, and hopefully Donovan would recognise her and they could be reunited. On 8 February 1916 she came to the city and was escorted by a member of the District Passenger Agent's Claims staff. Within an hour of the search, the two were together again – as the owner and accompanying member of staff entered a field on Heslington Lane, Donovan entered the same field from the other side, and after initially knocking his owner over in his excitement, he then commenced to lovingly lick her hand and the two were returned to York station. The *North Eastern Railway Magazine* reported that:

> Our clerk confesses to a feeling of great relief when he saw the lady seated in the train for Scarborough, with the dog under the seat, and himself without a scratch.

Fire at Tyne Dock

In January 1916 there was a severe fire at Tyne Dock, destroying a very large portion of the south-east quay. Owing to the war, the repairs were not of high priority but the damaged area was repaired and available for use again in 1918.

Snow storms

During the early days of March there were severe snow storms in the north-east, with lines temporarily blocked at Waskerley, Tow Law,

Rosedale and Annfield Plain. The Barnard Castle and Kirkby Stephen branch was the worst hit, and was believed to be the worst in this area for thirty years. Drifts were between ten and fifteen feet deep, but at Bleath Gill, near Stainmore Summit which at 1,370 feet was the highest point on any railway line in England, drifts were up to thirty feet deep. In this area the snow had started falling on 26 February, but trains had still managed to run until 11 March, but by this point even snow ploughs, large ploughs built on the chassis of old locomotive tenders, pushed by steam locomotives to ram the snow at speed to try and dislodge it, were of no use. On the 11 March, the 10.24 p.m. passenger train from Kirkby Stephen was stuck in a snow drift at Stainmore Summit and was not freed until 2.20 p.m. the next day. A mineral train was buried at Bleath Gill, and other mineral trains held up east of the summit. The storm continued until 14 March, and whilst the storm raged up to 385 men were brought together, joined by 150 men of the Durham Light Infantry who were used to clear the snow as it was a matter of national importance to keep trains running over this line. The remaining held up trains were released by 15 March, and service was back to normal by the next day.

Dairycoates Coaling Stage

A novel new piece of equipment came into use on 27 March 1916 at Dairycoates engine shed, Hull. In 1913 works were authorised to extent sidings and the engine shed at Dairycoates, and along with the extension to the engine shed it was decided to install a new type of coaling stage – a mechanical coaling stage, instead of the more common coaling staith where coal was dropped, or shovelled, from coal wagons on a railway line above and to the side of a locomotive on a special coaling stage into its tender or bunker. Although a mechanical coaling stage would cost a lot more to build, the initial cost of its building would be outweighed by that saved in working costs such as manual labour opposed to a coaling staith. The Dairycoates coaling stage was not the first in the country, as by the time of its opening they were also in use at Crewe North, Camden and Edge Hill by the London & North Western Railway, but it was a new feature for the North Eastern Railway. The saving of labour by this new coaling stage design was of particular important to the railway during the First World War when so many men had already left for the forces. The coaling stage worked by unloading the full coal wagons with a 'tipper', which literally tipped the wagon up to empty the coal inside through an opening end door into an underground hopper. A 'jigging screen' and 'coal breaker' broke the coal up on its way to the hopper and it was then brought up a central conveyor belt from the underground hopper to the top of the coaling stage, from where it was put into one of two bunkers, one of which held 100 tons of coal and the other 200 tons. The coal was then directed through a chute into the tenders or bunkers of the locomotives below.

Gifts for servicemen

Although not all North Eastern Railway men could join the forces during the First World War, owing to health reasons, age, or simply that they could not be spared from their vital railway work, those that stayed at home were eager to help the men that were fighting. By mid-1916 the men employed at Heaton and Walker Gate railway shops, prevented from joining the forces owing to their vital duties, had raised a large sum of money for wounded soldiers and sailors, widows, orphans, and Belgian refugees by various means. Subscriptions paid by the men from their wages totalled £479 from the locomotive department and £3 19 4s from the carriage and wagon department – as well as another £25 14s 3½d raised between 4 October 1914 and 20 April 1916 to provide comforts for wounded soldiers at Newcastle Infirmary. this money went towards 12,200 cigarettes, 1,410 bananas, 250 oranges, a large quantity of apples and also Christmas gifts of cake and chocolate. Another £61 for Belgian refugees was raised from a concert and street procession, another concert was held to raise funds for a soldiers and sailors hostel in Newcastle, a motor ambulance fund, and the Heaton Junction Ambulance Class. To top it off, a tea was held followed by entertainment put on for soldiers and sailors from the Newcastle Infirmary and Armstrong College (the turning over of large buildings such as schools and stately homes for use as hospitals was common) at the Heaton Road Congregational Hall. The men were transported by trams provided by the Newcastle

Tramways Department, and motor cars provided by the Chamber of Commerce Military Committee. During the evening's entertainment the men were given tobacco, cigarettes, cigars and fruit, to follow on from the previous tea.

Air Raids

Following the East Coast Bombardment which shelled the towns of, and affected the North Eastern Railway at, Hartlepool, Whitby and Scarborough in December 1914, the North Eastern Railway area also came under attack from Zeppelins from 1915 onwards. In total, during the war there were forty warnings of air raids to the North Eastern Railway's areas, twenty-three materialising into actual air raids. Of all the airship raids, none resulted in major disruption to the NER, mainly being limited to damage to telegraph wires, signal posts and glass used in buildings. The NER formed special fire brigades as part of the air raid defences at twenty-seven different locations, and also provided air raid shelters for both company staff and the general public, including using arches under railway lines at Hull, Loftus and York. The question of whether the railway should continue to operate during air raids was raised when the Zeppelin menace started to grow in 1915. If trains were to stop for the protection of staff and any public on the train, then ongoing delays to the service could cause further damage to the war effort than the effects of the raid itself. In April 1916 it was decided that in the event of a raid train services should still run but at reduced speeds, and for work in goods yards to continue with reduced lights to minimise the threat of an enemy aircraft using the lights as a guide for bombing. As well as those NER men killed during the East Coast Bombardment of December 1914, a further two members of NER staff were injured whilst on service during air raids. At least one member of staff and one pensioner were killed whilst off duty, both of these deaths occurring during the night of 2–3 May 1916 attack on York as well as the injury of the sister of the off-duty member of staff killed in the raid (as mentioned later in the chapter).

Hull received the brunt of the airship raids on NER territory, the first occurring on the night of 6–7 June 1915 when Zeppelin L9 raided the city, resulting in twenty-four dead. Imperial German Navy Zeppelin

L9 was commanded by Kapitänleutnant Heinrich Mathy, possibly the most well known Zeppelin commander, who was a household name in Britain for his frequent raids. The second raid on Hull occurred on the night of 5–6 March 1916 when Zeppelin L14 and Zeppelin L1 both attacked the city, both being blown south from targets further north up the coast. The first Zeppelin to attack, L14, made two bombing runs before having to return to base due to water freezing in the engines and St Elmo's Fire occurring on board (a weather phenomenon which gives off a bright light caused by a strong electrical atmosphere – not a good sign in a hydrogen filled airship). When L11 came on scene shortly after L14 left, attracted by the fires started by L14's bombs, the Zeppelin was able to easily rain destruction down onto the city, hovering steadily over it completely unmolested. Despite the attack the year before, Hull was defended by a single, dummy, wooden anti-aircraft gun – not much use even as a visual deterrence at night. Eighteen were killed and a further fifty injured. During the raid Hull Paragon station received a direct hit, damaging both the District Engineer's office and the Royal Station Hotel. Damage was also caused to the electric lighting installation of the station and the District Engineer's office. Over on the docks, No. 12 electric crane on Riverside Quay was severely damaged by bomb damage – the structure was buckled, part of the trolley wires were lost into the river, and the windows and controller were broken. The damage meant the entire crane was taken down, repaired and then re-erected, which was completed by November 1916.

Hull was to receive a further four visits from Zeppelins during the war – although the raid of 5–6 April did not result in a single bomb being dropped owing to newly introduced anti-aircraft guns following public pressure from the March raid, one person died of fright. The penultimate attack on the night of 24–25 September 1917 by Zeppelin L41 caused damage to the clock tower at Albert Dock, Hull.

On the night of 1–2 April two Imperial German Navy Zeppelins, L11 and L17, set off to bomb London – owing to weather they both diverted to northern England. L17 suffered engine failure around ten miles south east from Hornsea, where it had been circling whilst waiting for night to fall, and so dropped its bombs in the sea before returning home. L11 however came over land at Seaham Harbour at around 11.05 p.m., and commenced to drop twenty-seven bombs on the Sunderland area, before heading south to Middlesbrough for a smaller attack. The raid resulted in twenty two deaths and one hundred and thirty injuries, mainly in the Sunderland area. The raid also caused damage to the North Eastern Railway at Monkwearmouth – the store house used by the rulley repairers was completely demolished by a bomb, and caused considerable damage to the lean-to shed used to repair the rulley's. The Wagon Examiner's Cabin was also damaged by a direct hit on the boundary wall fifty yards away, which also wrecked the upper portion of the Engineers Signal Van. Damage was also caused to a North Eastern Railway covered goods wagon and a Great Northern Railway wagon. A carriage which formed part of the 9.48 p.m. train from South Shields received light damage – a panel being broken and requiring a side ducket light on the 3rd Class carriage to be repaired. Elsewhere in the goods yard, a bomb hit a warehouse causing skylights to break – the falling glass fell on the motor of an electric hoist in the warehouse, breaking the brake stopper and two electric brake wires and the glass covering the armature and commutator, putting it out of use.

On the night of 2–3 May 1916, York was to come under attack by a Zeppelin for the first of three times during the war. German Navy Zeppelin L21, commanded by Kapitänleutnant der Reserve Max Dietrich, approached York from the Bishopthorpe direction at 10.30 p.m., first dropping eighteen bombs on Dringhouses which injured two soldiers. The Zeppelin then flew over York itself from south-west to north-east, bombs dropping on Nunthorpe Hall Red Cross Hospital and Nunthorpe Avenue. A bomb dropped on Nunthorpe Avenue killed a young girl living there, at the same time injuring the spine of her sister and ripping an arm off her mother. Other bombs collapsed a house in Upper Price Street killing the elderly couple living there, the male a North Eastern Railway pensioner. Further bombs killed five civilians and one soldier. Amongst the civilian dead was a female typist in the employ of the North Eastern Railway. Her sister, also an NER typist, was seriously wounded. York was to be raided two further times during the year, on the night of 25–26 September by Zeppelin L14 and on the night of 27–28 November by L13. W. T. Naylor, a bricklayer at York Carriage Works and also a member of the North Eastern Railway fire brigade was to be awarded a medallion by the North Eastern Railway Centre of the St Johns Ambulance Association on 2 July 1917 at a meeting of the York City Council, for conspicuous bravery during one of the Zeppelin raids on York. His actions were described thus:

> Without hesitation he entered a house, amidst falling bricks, mortar *etc.* which had been severely damaged by a Zepp bomb and rescued three persons (two women and one man). He also rescued a woman from another house who had been severely injured by a piece of flying shell, rendering the necessary first aid and arranging for conveyance to hospital.

W. T. Naylor's son was in the army and had been awarded the Military Medal for bravery at the front. In the words of the Lord Mayor of York, this showed that "the family came from the right stock".

Scremerston derailment

The derailment of the 11.30 p.m. Down King's Cross to Edinburgh express early in the morning on 19 May, occurred on the approach to Scremerston station, three-and-a-half miles south of Berwick. The train, consisting of eight carriages and three vans, had been hauled by a North Eastern Railway 4-4-2 'Atlantic' express locomotive since Newcastle, driven by Henry Oswald Pennington, and had left Newcastle at 5.01 a.m., two minutes late. On the approach to Scremerston station at a speed of between 50 and 60 mph, he heard a loud 'crack' that gave him the impression of the leading tender axle breaking. As soon as he heard the noise he shut off steam and applied the brake, as his first impression seemed to be confirmed from the riding of the tender, which then suddenly changed to give the impression that the whole tender was off the rails. He could not tell if any of the train was off the rails owing to the coal being thrown off the tender by the oscillations, but judged that there were other vehicles derailed from the 'pull' on the tender.

One of the guards on the train, James Shepphard who was in the joint employ of the North Eastern Railway and Great Northern Railway as he worked on the East Coast line, was riding in the van behind the tender and first noticed something wrong when the brakes were applied, and shortly after the parcels started to tumble over him. He then heard something strike the side of the van, likely to be the platform sides at Scremerston station. Sheppard had to hang on to the side partition of the van until it stopped as the van jolted until it came to a stop. At the rear of the train though, Guard Martin Young noticed the brakes being applied but had no idea of the derailment until the train came to a stop. The locomotive came to a stop just opposite the north end of the platform, with the locomotive still on the rails whilst the tender and seven leading vehicles were derailed to the left of the line, with the seventh vehicle's leading bogie derailed but the rear bogie still on the line. All parts of the train from locomotive to rearmost vehicle were still coupled together and standing upright, and despite carrying 175 passengers, fortunately not a single injury. The four leading carriages were damaged from fouling the station platform as well as slight damage to the tender. When Driver Pennington inspected the tender, despite the sound and actions of the tender leading him to believe the leading axle had broken on the tender wheels, they were intact.

Inspections by George Logan, the Carriage & Wagon Examiner, found that there was nothing wrong with any of the carriages or vans that could have caused the derailment, they were all right to gauge and there were no bent axles, and were fine to be taken away in their condition once new axleboxes were fitted to some. The inspection of the locomotive and tender by Divisional Locomotive Superintendent C. Baister found that there was an internal flaw in the front hanger of the left hand leading spring for the tender's wheels, and it had broken off. The hanger was a vertical piece of metal, one-and-seven-eighths of an inch in diameter and made of wrought-iron, and there were two for each set of springs, one on each side. These would 'hang' the weight of the tender on to the springs which were mounted on the outside of the tender's chassis frames. The springs transferred the weight of the tender through the axlebox and on to the axle and wheels, the end of the axles as the name suggests sitting in an axlebox on each side of the tender. The breakage of a hanger therefore meant the weight of the tender resting on that side of the axle was completely relieved, whilst at the other end of the axle it would remain as the hangers were still in place, and the uneven distribution of weights would cause the wheels to derail. The uneven running this caused of the tender in turn caused the centre spring on the left hand side of the tender to work loose also, causing the middle axle to derail, and then the rearmost axle to derail.

The part that had broken off was not found despite inspection of the railway line along where it was presumed to have come off.

As the tender was derailed and the wheels were dragged along underneath the tender, the tender derailed to the left of the railway line and so wheels on the right hand side of the wheel fouled the wooden sleepers set in between the railway, causing severe damage. When the tender reached a set of points the wheels wrecked the track work in the middle of the rails, which broke a rail and derailed the seven vehicles behind the tender. Fortunately this did not derail more as the train was brought to a halt before the rearmost bogie of the seventh vehicle was derailed. Divisional Superintendent Baister mentioned that as it was an internal flaw it would have been very hard to detect, and the only possible way the it could have been detected was if the hanger was entirely removed. The hanger was covered by a bracket, and bolts holding it would have to be slacked off and the bracket and hanger taken off, which was not a usual inspection. Although Baister had seen broken hangers before, it was a very rare occurrence and was not aware of any derailment due to a broken hanger before. The locomotive and tender had undergone a thorough overhaul the previous year and left the works on 31 March 1915, and had been in for repairs between the 2 and 25 March 1916, but for repairs to the engine only. The recommendations of the enquiry found that the current type of hanger had been in use for years, and although breakages were very rare and had not caused a derailment before, the crash had proved they did have the capability to do so. The North Eastern Railway was advised that it should consider if any improvement could be made to strengthen the hanger and/or to facilitate the inspection of the hangers.

Dining carriages

Owing to the war, from 1 May onwards, dining and restaurant cars on the North Eastern Railway, which included East Coast services between London and Scotland, were withdrawn from service for the duration of war. As well as the difficulties the railway was facing with staff shortages meaning staff used for these carriages could be put to much better use elsewhere, it was no doubt also considered bad form for such luxurious services to still be offered in time of global conflict.

Croft Spa derailment

A derailment at Croft Spa on 14 June caused a passenger train hauled by M1 Class 4-4-0 express passenger locomotive 1625 to crash into a derailed train of wagons – the force of the impact of the locomotive crashing into a wagon caused it to come off the rails and lie almost on its side, tearing up the rails and the ground beneath them. Either of the trains possibly contained military equipment, as armed soldiers are evident in photographs of the crash guarding the wreckage.

A Poaching 'Special'

An amusing incident occurred on 10 July involving the engineer's special train from York to West Hartlepool, hauled by one 190 Class 2-2-4T locomotives No. 167. When the train arrived at West Hartlepool, a cock pheasant was found tightly wedged in the end 'link' of the chain coupling at the front of the engine, facing forwards. It was believed that the pheasant must have been running between the rails as the train approached, and rose from the rails just as the train started to overtake it, catching it with some force in the chain coupling. It is not mentioned whether the pheasant was dead or not, but the force of the impact and following journey at relatively high speed cannot have done it much good.

Submarine attack

North Eastern Railway territory was to come under attack from the sea for the first time since the east coast bombardment of 1914 on 11 July 1916 (there was also a raid on Great Yarmouth and Lowestoft on 24 April, killing four civilians, wounding nineteen and a further twenty one naval personnel killed on Royal Navy warships intervening). A German U-boat surfaced off the small undefended port of Seaham on the Durham coast at 10.30 p.m., approaching the Harbour under cover at night, and then fired around thirty shells from its deck-mounted gun, twenty falling towards Dalton-de-Dale and twelve around Seaham Colliery. There was one casualty of the raid, a woman who was walking through the colliery yard was injured by a shell and died of her injuries on the morning of 12 July. Damage was light, one house was struck, a railway wagon carrying timber was hit and there was damage to a chimney in a pit yard – the damage was so light that it was deemed worth mentioning in news reports that several windows were broken and a shell landing in a field ploughed grass and made a large hole. The majority of the shells appeared to have been fired too high and simply fell harmlessly about a-mile-and-a half inland.

North Eastern Railway employees save lives – and another employee drowns

In August, the clerk at Robin Hood's Bay station, Miss Olive M Parnaby, daughter of the station master, was involved in a life-saving incident when a lady fell off the Scaur (a series of rocks jutting out into the sea), and also two lady bathers who had got out of their depths, one of them fainting. Miss Parnaby, only sixteen-and-a-half years old at the time, was a natural swimmer and brought them all safely ashore. She had been acting as clerk since November 1915, presumably to make up for staff shortages owing to the war. Another saving of life from drowning by a North Eastern Railway employee in that month, on 8 August, when Charles Hall, a fitter in the Engineer's Department was working with others on repairing the "Cloughs" near the Flour Mill in Boroughbridge. Hall had observed two boys bathing in the water above the weir there, and noticed that they had got into difficulties. He at once went to their rescue, bringing them both back to dry land – this was not the first time Hall had saved someone from drowning, in 1910 he saved a man whilst at Blackpool.

Unfortunately the next month was to see a North Eastern Railway man drown – John Phillips joined the Royal Scots Fusiliers whilst aged 17, and then after transfer to the Royal Engineers served through the Second Boer War. After the Second Boer War he was transferred to the Reserve until he was called up on the outbreak of war and went back to the front in October 1914, before being invalided home in March 1915 after an attack of rheumatism. Back in the UK he was put on home service at Chatham in Kent until March 1916 when he was transferred to work at the North Eastern Railway locomotive works at Gateshead employed on munitions work. He was on holiday at Whitley Bay when he sadly drowned on 1 September.

Death of Lieutenant G. S. Kaye Butterworth

A serious blow came to General Manager Sir Alexander Kaye Butterworth in 1916 – his only son, Lieutenant George Sainton Kaye Butterworth MC of the 13th Battalion Durham Light Infantry was killed on 5 August during the Battle of the Somme. Lieutenant Butterworth was educated at Eton and was a well-known composer, best known for 'The Banks of Green Willow'. At the start of the war he enlisted as a Private in the Duke of Cornwall's Light Infantry but was soon given a commission in the Durham Light Infantry, working alongside many Durham miners whom he much admired. He was awarded the Military Cross for his actions in capturing German trenches near Pozieres on 16–17 July, commanding a Company of men as a temporary Lieutenant from 17 to 19 July. On the night of 4–5 August he was taking part in a bombing attack on a German trench with his Company of men, leading the attack from the front which led to his death when the trench they captured came under heavy fire from German bombs and shells. His body was never recovered and is now one of 72,191 men listed on the Thiepval Memorial with no known grave.

New offices

New offices were built for the North Eastern Railway in Sunderland in 1916, and named Burdon House. The magnificent four storey offices were for the District Superintendent's staff in the business centre of Sunderland adjacent to the public park, with the street level shops being rented out to private firms, as well as any spare rooms in the building. One innovative design of the building was an electric lift for those working inside the building.

Cannons

An amusing photograph and caption was published in the October issue of the *North Eastern Railway Magazine*, showing ancient-looking cannons which would have appeared more at home on a warship at the Battle of Trafalgar over a century before. The accompanying text described the weapons:

> We reproduce a photograph of the station staff at Kirbymoorside who had just unloaded from a Great Eastern truck some old German guns, formerly used against the natives in West Africa. They were presented to Captain Fuller, CMG, DSO, RN, of Kirbymoorside who took a prominent part in the operations against the Germans in the Cameroons and for his services there has been awarded three decorations. Mr J. T. Forster, to whom we are indebted for the illustration, writes – "It is to be hoped that the Magazine will not get into the hands of the Germans, or they may take it for granted that Kirbymoorside is a fortified place".

A death on the line

Another industrial accident occurred on the North Eastern Railway on 4 October when the chargeman platelayer, Sherwood Dawson, was run over and immediately killed by a passenger train whilst on the line near Tees Bridge signal box. He was a much liked and respected member of staff who had worked on the North Eastern Railway since 1879 and had been chargeman since 27 May 1906.

More wartime regulations

13 December saw a new regulation made under the Defence of the Realm Act, Regulation 7B, which was to apply to the British railways: 7b – 1) The Board of Trade may, for the purpose of making the most efficient use of railway plant or labour, with a view to the successful prosecution of the war, make orders for all or any of the following purposes, namely –

(a) For enabling the Board of Trade to take possession of any private owner's wagons and to use those wagons in such manner as they think best in the interests of the country, as a whole, on such conditions as to payment, use and otherwise as may be provided by the order;

(b)   For enforcing the prompt loading or unloading of wagons, by making failure to load or unload in accordance with the order an offence;

(c)   For curtailing any statutory requirements as to the running of trains or affording other facilities on certain lines or at certain stations or for requiring the disuse of any such line or station, in cases where the curtailment or disuse appears to the Board of Trade to be justified by the necessity of the case;

(d)   For restricting or prohibiting certain classes of traffic (including the carriage of passengers' luggage) on railways either absolutely or subject to any conditions for which provision is made by the order;

(e)   For modifying any statutory requirements with respect to the maximum amount of passenger fares
(2) If any person acts in contravention of or fails to comply with any of the provisions of an order so made he shall be guilty of a summary offence against these regulations
(3) Any order may be made so as to apply generally to all railways or to any class of railways or to any special railway
(4) Any order of the Board of Trade under the regulation may be revoked, extended, or varied as occasion required.

1917

1917 had barely begun when an enormous explosion at the Silvertown Munitions Works devastated a large area of the east end of London, killing seventy-three and injuring over four hundred. The Zeppelin raids on London were replaced with aeroplane raids, much harder to detect and shoot down and proving more deadly, killing over one thousand civilians. The raids took place almost entirely through the night as one bomber aircraft would attack, followed by another and another. On the Western Front, the Battle of Arras occurred in the spring, followed by the Battle of Messines Ridge and then the 3rd Battle of Ypres in the summer, soon affected by unseasonal rainfall which turned the battlefield into a quagmire. The Battle of Cambrai in late 1917 proved that the new tanks, used en-masse, could make large advances into German territory, although German counter-attacks re-took most of the land gained, and the chance would not come again until August 1918. In April 1917 the United States of America declared war on Germany; however, it took time to equip and train its army for war. The Russian Revolution which started in February with the overthrow of the Tsar, took Russia out of the war in November. The first, second and third Battles of Gaza in Palestine took place against the Ottoman Empire, the first two ended in failure, but the third resulted in the capture of Gaza, with Jerusalem taken in December.

Winter problems

The winter of 1916–17 was a harsh one – S. Cooper, traffic agent at Rosedale goods station high on the North Yorkshire Moor thought that it had 'I think, been the worst experienced in the history of the railway'. The first snow fell on 18 November 1916, and he reckoned it had fallen most days until at least 18 April 1917 – this included a spell of the line, only used for mineral traffic, being completely blocked from 8 January until 12 February. This was despite the efforts of snowploughs and two powerful locomotives attempting to clear them. The snowploughs were in use most days since the snow storm commenced, with drifts of up to thirty feet at Blakey Junction, and four feet deep drifts being dealt with through to April. The Rosedale Branch was exceptional as it was one of the highest lines on the North Eastern Railway network going up to 1,370 feet above sea level.

The year was to start on a sad note for the North Eastern Railway, as on 5 January popular member of staff John W. Bradbury was killed in an accident during shunting operations at Neville Hill Sidings in Leeds, aged just twenty-seven.

Recognition for Raven

Following his hard work for the war effort, the New Year Honours List, published on 13 February, included a very well-known name to the staff of the North Eastern Railway – Vincent L. Raven, the Chief Mechanical Engineer.

Locomotives

Early 1917 was to bring in a change of appearance to the North Eastern Railway – as a concession to the war effort, a more utilitarian livery was adopted for the goods and mineral locomotives – from 1904 they had been painted in a different colour from the passenger locomotives, in black with vermillion lining and 'N.E.R.' in gold lettering along the tender side. The locomotive's number was on a large brass cabside plate with the location and date of manufacture on it. From March 1917 this became a more austere all-over black, with a much smaller cabside plate. The number was painted on the tender, flanked by the letters 'N' before and 'E' after – the livery was to stay until the end of the company, when it was grouped with other railway companies in 1923 to become the London and North Eastern Railway. (Interestingly, during the Second World War a similar 'austerity' livery would come into effect for all locomotives, plain black again, with just 'NE' on the tender.) Fortunately this was the only concession in livery for the North Eastern Railway during the war, as the beautiful green livery lined in black and white used on the passenger locomotives was kept throughout, even on the newly built Z1 Atlantic locomotives.

As described in the 'On War Service' chapter, the contribution to the war effort of the entire class of 50 T1 Class 0-8-0 locomotives was made in early 1917. This very generous contribution left a serious dent in the locomotive availability of the North Eastern Railway, leaving the T and T2 Class 0-8-0 locomotives and smaller 0-6-0 locomotives to cope with a traffic load increased above pre-war levels. As a form of compensation from the Government for the T1 Class, materials were made available to the company to build locomotives to replace them, and in April 1917 the first of the new batch of T2s came into service, No. 2213. In all, forty T2 Class locomotives were built, numbered 2213–2252, and all were built at Darlington – nineteen were built in total in 1917, followed by eight in 1918 (including No. 2238 which was completed in October 1918, now preserved by the North Eastern Locomotive Preservation Group) and thirteen in 1919.

The original two orders for what was to become these two batches of twenty T2 Class locomotives had been placed in 1914. The order and numbers allocated for locomotives 2233–2242 were for a batch of twenty D Class 4-4-4T express passenger tank engines, designed for hauling express services over short distances. The orders had been put on hold owing to the war and were subsequently changed to the T2 Class as it was felt that these would be more useful in wartime. Locomotive production had slowed during the war, but not stopped completely – at the start of the war, construction of a batch of twenty E1 Class 0-6-0T tank engines was in progress and completed in September, the latest of a highly successful design first built in 1898, of which 113 in total were built across nine batches, the last batch of eight being built as late as 1951. The war did of course mean that the amount of locomotives built did slow down, and required that older locomotives were kept in service longer than planned, such as the 901 Class 2-4-0 passenger engines, first built in 1882, and the 1001 Class locomotives, which were originally a Stockton & Darlington Railway design. The rate of retirements of locomotives slowed down drastically during the war – in 1914, forty-eight locomotives were withdrawn from traffic, in 1915 this went down to sixteen, in 1916 just two (the same amount of locomotives that were built in that year), seven in 1917 and five in 1918. In 1919 the number went up to thirty-six, helped by the return of locomotives that were assisting with the war effort and the increased production of new locomotives.

The only locomotives to be built throughout the war were the Z1 Class 'Atlantic' express passenger engines, with ten built in 1914, twelve in 1915, just two in 1916, going up to four in 1917 and just the one in 1918. The Z1 Class 'Atlantic' locomotives, with a 4-4-2 wheel arrangement and used for fast passenger services were built by the North British Locomotive Company in 1911, with them building ten Z Class with saturated boilers and ten Z1 Class with superheated boilers. The Z1 proved more successful and building commenced again for delivery in 1914 at Darlington, and in 1914–15 the ten Z Class locomotives were converted into the superheated Z1 Class. Despite the reduction in staff and higher demands placed on the railway, the North Eastern Railway managed to continue to maintain their locomotives and rolling stock to a high standard, and were even kept looking clean and very presentable, which was certainly helped by the army of women cleaners who were employed on the railway during the war.

Entertainment for wounded soldiers

On Saturday 10 March 1917, entertainment was put on at the North Eastern Railway Institute in Gateshead by the railwaymen at the nearby locomotive workshops, who themselves could not join owing to their vital work. This group of railwaymen had already given a great deal of time and money to those who served as mentioned in the previous chapter, and it continued throughout the war. Seventy-five sick and injured soldiers from the Bensham Hospital were entertained with a 'knife and fork tea' followed by a dance and social, paid for by a subscription of over £18 raised by the enginemen. The billiard and games rooms in the Institute were taken full advantage of and as at previous entertainment put on by the railwaymen, there was an ample supply of cigarettes, fruit, chocolate and other refreshment. Some of the servicemen were "able to entertain as well as to be entertained and proved talented singers". It was a great success and hot on the heels, another evening double the size was already being planned for the Easter Monday. At the same time it was reported that J. W. Bentley, a fireman at Gateshead, had lost two of his four sons who had joined the forces. One, Private Robert Bentley, worked at Gateshead Locomotive works as hammer lad from 1908 until 1912 and was killed in 1914. Another of his sons, Private Henry Bentley, who was a machine lad at the locomotive works before joining up, was wounded, and Sapper James Bentley was an apprentice boilersmith at Gateshead locomotive works and had been at the front for two years at the time of writing in early 1917. Another son, Joseph Bentley, was working at Gateshead Locomotive Works and had been since 1902. His fifth son, who was killed in action in 1915, did not have previous North Eastern Railway service.

Allotments

The North Eastern Railway had provided allotments for many years already, having around 7,000 on company land by the outbreak of war. With food shortages having more and more of an effect as the war went on, many called for the public to make better use of allotments to grow vegetables or keep small animals – the North Eastern Railway was among those, and a notice going out in the *North Eastern Railway Magazine* at the start of 1917 stated;

> It is imperative, therefore, both for his own and the country's sake, that every man who can should cultivate an allotment.

The Land Cultivation Committee was set up to manage allotments, by this stage of the war there being about 10,000 North Eastern Railway men growing food in free line-side gardens, gardens attached to North Eastern Railway owned houses, or in paid allotments on North Eastern Railway land. The allotments were free to rent, after an initial agreement was signed with a six penny stamp to protect the North Eastern Railway from damage. From now on, to help encourage people to take up an allotment, the North Eastern Railway would supply the stamp, as well as making new allotments where possible. These allotments would be made available to railway staff at first, and then the general public. Books were suggested, and the highly recommended A. S. Galt's *Making and Management of an Allotment* was offered for free by the North Eastern Railway. For the rest of the war, a large portion of the *North Eastern Railway Magazine* was devoted to allotments and tips for growing food or managing animals and insects. By February 1917 there were already 1,150 additional allotments (including line-side gardens) taken up since the start of the appeal.

The North Eastern Railway had arranged for 1 cwt bags of potato seed to be delivered carriage free to any station on their network – each bag cost 15 shillings, and allowing for other vegetables to be grown on an allotment, there was enough seed in one bag for two 300 square yard plots. Garden allotment Associations were also set up in various districts to help out at a more local level. One thorny subject was that of buildings on allotments – they were considered "rather an eyesore", especially as they were mostly poorly built wooden structures, often with old enamel advertisement signs to patch them up. However, they were sometimes necessary, for use as tool sheds or to house animals such as chickens or goats, and so although the North Eastern Railway would not give consent to building on allotments, they would not stop them unless they caused or resulted in an eyesore or nuisance to the railway, adjoining tenants or the outside public. A 'nuisance' in this instance included unsightly or untidy buildings, insufficiently protected hen houses/runs or rabbit hutches, unduly shading adjoining allotments preventing growth there, or crowing cockerels in the vicinity of houses. Those wanting to erect buildings were advised to consult the secretary of the local allotment association, if there was one, as to suitable buildings.

Goats were particularly encouraged, and there were many correspondents to the *North Eastern Railway Magazine* extolling their virtues – this was led by A. S. Umbleby, the stationmaster at Moss station, who started a regular column under the title 'Goat keeping by railwaymen', later shortened to 'Goat notes'. As well as suitable for allotments, goats were also suitable for being kept on the railway line-side, as long as they were suitably tethered. The average female goat would produce six pints daily after kidding, falling to one pint a day after eight months, and so three goats were recommended for an all year round supply. During the summer they could be fed on vegetable and garden waste and so were very economical to keep. In the words of A. S. Umbleby, "there are few animals so profitable and also few animals so little appreciated" as the goat. In May 1917 it was announced the North Eastern Railway would advance £2 10s towards the price of purchasing a goat, repayable at one shilling per week – a very generous offer. Kids were available from just five shillings, and a one-year-old goat costing between thirty shillings and £2, and they were able to be mated at fifteen to eighteen months old. The North Eastern Railway Goat Club was started in July 1917, and the influence of the 'goat notes' extended far beyond the the north east of England – one British Army officer, formerly of the North Eastern Railway, wrote in to the magazine from Mesopotamia to say that the regular column was of great use to him, as his unit had two goats they had 'acquired' for milking.

Rabbit was also recommended by the Board of Agriculture for eating, and chickens were also popular – the North Eastern Railway was not the only railway company encouraging its staff, and the public, to be more self-supporting with food – the Great Central Railway had a 'poultry train' which toured the system giving demonstrations on chicken keeping with public addresses and also explanations of all aspects of poultry keeping. The 'poultry train' was lent to the North Eastern Railway in the spring of 1917, spending March in Yorkshire, opening in Scarborough on 15 March with an attendance of 1,616, and the average attendance over seven Yorkshire railway stations was 1,419. The train ran through Northumberland and Durham in April and May, half of the attendances at railway stations were to coincide with that town's market day.

Articles continued with the seasonal variations which would affect allotments and how best to utilise them – bee keeping was another subject for articles. An unexpected home for bees was created at Goathland railway station in June 1917 when a swarm made a new home in a water crane used to refill the water tanks of the steam locomotives, and the unenviable task of removing them had to be undertaken. The humble cabbage got one North Eastern Railway man in trouble – he had torn the name of a type of cabbage, the 'Blackwell Early', out of a copy of the Magazine and had left it lying around whilst he went to get seeds for this variant. In his absence, a woman cleaning up (possibly his wife) found the piece of paper, and upon his return accused him of being "nothing better than a 'horse-race gambler'", it taking him some time to convince her that it was in fact a cabbage and not the name of a horse or horse race that he then went out to fritter away his money gambling on!

By March 1918 it was reported that there were now 11,151 allotments on the North Eastern Railway, and allotment holders associations were proving popular. By the end of the war, there were 16,969 allotments on North Eastern Railway land, an increase of almost 10,000 since the outbreak of war. The driving force of the articles on allotments was John Howe, who joined the North Eastern Railway in 1880 and was an engine driver in the Darlington district during the war until early 1918 when he was appointed locomotive inspector.

Civilian railway workers at the front

With the increasing amount of railway lines being built for the Railway Operating Division on the Western Front, the Railway Executive Committee asked the large railway companies for men for three months' service in constructing railways. The North Eastern Railway's appeal for volunteers was extremely well received, with a full North Eastern Railway unit of 250 men made, and an additional 89 men who went to a composite unit of men from other companies. The 250-man-unit left York together on 15 March 1917 on a special train after an address from the General Manager and Chief Engineer and arrived in France just two days later. R. R. Woodward of the Chief Engineer's Office was the engineer-in-charge of the North Eastern Railway unit, assisted by W. J. Newbald, A. G. Cape, J. A. Stuart and O. P. Kennedy. In total, the unit was made up of:

1 Senior Engineer
2 Junior Engineers
1 Surveyor
1 Draughtsman

1 Cashier
1 Clerk
1 Permanent Way Inspector
4 Foremen
8 Gangers
16 Sub-gangers
185 Platelayers
6 Blacksmiths
10 Carpenters
2 Storekeepers
1 Timekeeper
4 Timbermen
2 Signal locking fitters
2 Motor cyclists
2 Cooks
The 89 other men for the composite unit left York on 29 March.

Deaths of railwaymen

W. J. Smith, a locomotive fireman of the North Eastern Railway at Bridlington, met an unfortunate end on 12 August whilst walking along cliffs when he was struck by lightning and killed. He was aged twenty-six and had been with the railway for seven years. He was a well-known and respected man and noted for his considerable religious work. Later that month another North Eastern Railway man was killed but this time whilst on duty – W. B. McGregor who was the station locomotive foreman at York station was knocked down by the locomotive of a passenger train on 18 August. He was fifty-eight and been with the railway since May 1873.

Scarborough attacked again

Scarborough was the victim of seaborne attack on the morning of 4 September, this time from a German submarine rather than warships – it appeared that the intended target were the armed minesweepers working in the bay, and after they started to return fire the U-boat soon disappeared below the surface of the sea, after a bombardment of around ten to fifteen minutes. Approximately thirty rounds were fired, with about half landing on the town itself, killing three and injuring six. This time there was no damage to the North Eastern Railway.

Catterick Camp Military Railway

The Catterick Camp Military Railway was built to serve the large camp built at Catterick in north Yorkshire, of which construction started in 1915 – it was operated by the military, but used North Eastern Railway rolling stock and locomotives. The camp opened in October 1916, and the four-and-a-half-mile branch line was so busy it even had its own locomotive allocated to help deal with traffic (see the chapter 'On War Service'). Unfortunately, an accident occurred on 15 September 1917 which resulted in the deaths of four soldiers and left forty-six more injured. Between 400–500 soldiers were boarding a train at the Catterick Camp station, the carriages of which were standing in the station alone without a locomotive attached. The carriages began to move, with not all the men in the carriages, and some of those that were already on board jumped out, realising something was wrong, however most stayed seated. The line featured a steep gradient, sloping downwards from the camp station – it was estimated that at one point the carriages had reached the speed of 60 mph. At one of the level crossings on the line, the rear coach derailed, and at a sharp curve the leading coach became detached from the rest of the train. The lone carriage ran forward for a further two miles until it reached the junction with the main North Eastern Railway line, where it derailed, knocked over a buffer stop and came to rest on the ballast of the railway line. The men in this carriage only received minor injuries, but upon leaving the carriage, minutes later Private Hugh Cameron was run down by the engine of a train being shunted at the junction, and died of his injuries. The second coach derailed and rolled down an embankment into a field, and the four other carriages that made up the train also received damage and the men inside received injuries. The uninjured soldiers went to the aid of those that were hurt, extracting men from the wreckage, and also sent for help. Before long a North Eastern Railway breakdown gang was on the way, and motor ambulances took the injured to military hospitals in the area. Two others were killed in the crash, Lance Corporal Pepper and Private Green, and a fourth, Private Muirhead, died of injuries two days later. The inquest found that Lance Corporal Wilson of the Royal Engineers, who was in charge of the train the day before, had left the train with the brakes on but was not able to lock the door to the guard's compartment of the brake van as the key was lost. No one was seen to have tampered with the brakes and the Colonel in charge of the soldiers who were on the train said no one had entered the brake van – he did mention a previous occurrence when a soldier had turned a brake wheel, releasing the brakes, not realising what it was. The only theory the Coroner could put forward was that a German prisoner of war held nearby may have escaped and released the brakes, but admitted this was highly unlikely. The verdict given was that of accidental death. As well as the four fatalities and numerous injuries, three carriages were completely wrecked and a further one condemned to destruction.

Women to war

Not just men of the North Eastern Railway left to join the military – on 5 October, Maud Spedding left the railway to join the Women's Auxiliary Army Corps. The WAAC was a unit formed in 1917 to provide women for non-combatant work such as driving, administration and cooking both in Britain and in France. As a gesture of goodwill, she was presented with a leather attaché case by the Carting Office staff at Newcastle Forth station.

New locomotive designs

In November 1917 and in June 1918 meetings were held by the Association of Railway Mechanical Engineers attended by the Chief Mechanical Engineers of most of the railways in Great Britain to discuss the possibility of three standard classes of locomotives to be built across all railways – the categories for the engine classes would be passenger, goods and mineral. The CME of the North Eastern Railway, Vincent Raven, was unable to attend due to his war work with the

1. Armband believed to have been temporarily issued to North Eastern Railway workers to show they were on railway service when not in uniform, to prove they were not shirking their duty, later worn by female workers to show they were allowed on railway property. (Author's collection)

2. E.RY marking on the base of an 18 Pounder shell that had passed through the North Eastern Railway-run Darlington National Projectile Factory. (Author's collection)

3. Talbot armoured car used by Lieutenant Wells-Hood, formerly of the North Eastern Railway. (*NER Magazine* 1914)

4. Small enamel badge worn by North Eastern Railway workers when not in uniform, which replaced the armbands – identical badges were issued by other railways. (Author's collection)

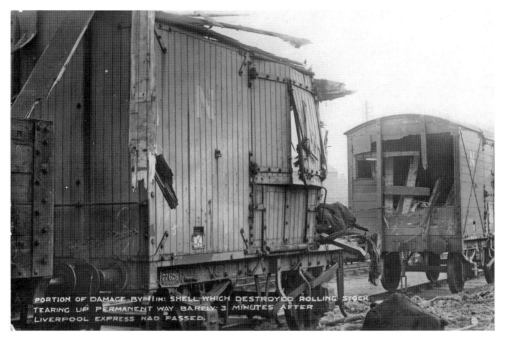

PORTION OF DAMAGE BY IIin: SHELL WHICH DESTROYED ROLLING STOCK TEARING UP PERMANENT WAY BARELY 3 MINUTES AFTER LIVERPOOL EXPRESS HAD PASSED.

5. Postcard showing damage to North Eastern Railway wagons caused by German shells during the bombardment of the Hartlepools in December 1914. (Author's collection)

6. Electric freight locomotive (in photographic grey, in service they were black lined in red) built for use on the Shildon to Newport line, opened in 1915. (Author's collection)

7. North Eastern Railway Maudslay and Leyland lorries, formerly buses and charabancs, converted at the Carriage & Wagon Works at York for use by the War Department. (*NER Magazine* 1914)

8. 18 pounder shrapnel shell as made at the Darlington National Projectile Factory – the brass case itself was repaired at the 'shell shop'. (Author's collection)

9. Female munitions workers, also known as 'munitionettes', of the Darlington National Projectile Factory. (Darlington Borough Council)

10. The wreckage of O Class 0-4-4T locomotive 1867 and E1 Class 0-6-0T 2182 following the St Bede's Junction crash of 17 December 1915. (Copyright unknown)

11. A Class 2-4-2T locomotive 671, the third locomotive to be involved in the St Bede's Junction crash. The coal bunker can be seen shorn away at the rear of the locomotive. (Copyright unknown)

12. M1 Class 4-4-0 1625 derailed in an accident at Croft Spa, 14 June 1916. (Copyright unknown)

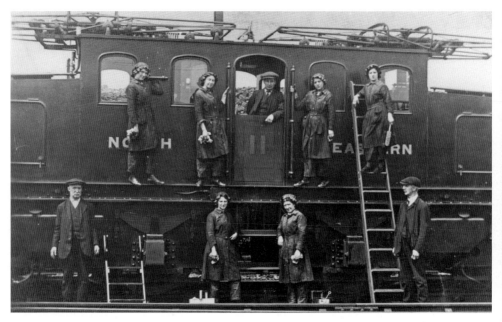

13. Female cleaners and male staff at Shildon with one of the Shildon-Newport electric freight locomotives, No. 11, in 1917. (Copyright unknown)

14. One of three North Eastern Railway single deck Leyland motor buses built in 1914, BT1508 is seen here at some point in the war having been converted to run on gas. (Copyright unknown)

15. One of two L Class 0-6-0T locomotives, 544, fitted with two Westinghouse pumps and used to move railway guns on the north east coast of the UK. (Copyright unknown)

16. T1 Class 0-8-0 locomotive 527, seen on Railway Operating Division service at St Omer, France *c.* 1917-18. (Copyright unknown)

17. Z1 Class 4-4-2 'Atlantic' locomotive 2207, built in 1917, at York. (Copyright unknown)

18. North Eastern Railway Hallford motor parcels van of 1908 seen in use as a 'ration van' delivering supplies to the 17th (North Eastern Railway) Northumberland Fusiliers whilst on coastal defence duties on the East Yorkshire coast. (*NER Magazine* 1915)

19. A Ford Model T van, requisitioned from 'City Garage' (which city is unknown) also on service to the 17th (North Eastern Railway) Northumberland Fusiliers. (*NER Magazine* 1915)

20. Inspection of the 17th Northumberland Fusiliers by North Eastern Railway Directors, 19th February 1915. (*NER Magazine* 1915)

21. 'The Railwayman as a Soldier' – By W. Lee of Newcastle. (*NER Magazine* 1915)

22. Women porters at Middlesbrough station. (*NER Magazine* 1915)

23. The North Eastern Railway tug *Stranton*, later known as HMS *Stranton* and lost in January 1915. (*NER Magazine* 1915)

24. The Sailors' and Soldiers' Buffet at York station, which proved popular throughout the war. (*NER Magazine* 1915)

25. North Eastern Railway Shell Shop – the hydraulic banding press. (*NER Magazine* 1916)

26. Overall view of the Darlington National Projectile Factory, also known as the North Eastern Railway Shell Shop. (*NER Magazine* 1916)

27. Lieutenant-Commander W. Wells-Hood. (*NER Magazine* 1916)

28. Wells-Hood, second from right, with a Rolls Royce armoured car in Russia. (*NER Magazine* 1916)

29. Shell Shop Bond Store. (*NER Magazine* 1916)

30. The first electric mineral train on the Shildon to Newport line, 1 July 1915. (*NER Magazine* 1916)

31. P2 or P3 Class locomotive being cleaned by women at Blaydon. (*NER Magazine* 1917)

32. The North Eastern Railway Ambulance Train of 1917. (*NER Magazine* 1917)

33. Carriage cleaners at Harrogate. (*NER Magazine* 1917)

34. North Eastern Railway Policewomen. (*NER Magazine* 1918)

35. Roll of Honour which appeared in a 1918 edition of the *NER Magazine*. (*NER Magazine* 1918)

36. Darlington War Workers decorated cart for the procession encouraging more women to join the war effort in 1918. (*NER Magazine* 1918)

37. 54 ton trolley wagon built by the North Eastern Railway at Gateshead in just eleven days in 1914. (*NER Magazine* 1919)

38. Side view of T1 Class locomotive 5660, originally 660 in North Eastern Railway service, as it served on the Western Front painted grey. (*NER Magazine* 1919)

Ministry of Munitions and so acting CME Arthur Stamer attended on behalf of both the North Eastern Railway and the Great Northern Railway, as Nigel Gresley was also unable to attend. This forward-thinking idea unfortunately did not result in any standard classes (this would not be attempted until after the formation of British Railways in 1948 when 'Standard Class' locomotives were designed and built to various power categories and for different uses). However, the meetings did result in George Heppell, the Chief Draughtsman of the North Eastern Railway, being asked to look into the design of three standard classes of locomotives, ideally with duplication of parts where possible for standardisation between the three. This was something not done by the South Eastern & Chatham Railway as noted by Heppell when their Chief Draughtsman visited him to compare designs. Of the three designs, two were built and entered service – the mineral locomotive was the T3 Class, an 0-8-0 three cylinder tender engine, and five were ordered in May 1918. Owing to the war it was not until October 1919 that the first completed T3 left Darlington Works, number 901 which is now preserved nearby at Darlington North Road Museum. The goods engine was to be the S3, a 4-6-0 which was successfully used for many years on both goods and passenger traffic. The first order for the S3 Class was placed in November 1918, but again did not enter service until 1919. The passenger engine design was designated the S4 but was never built – despite Heppell's confidence about the design it is unlikely that it would have compared well with the large passenger express locomotives later built by the North Eastern Railway and then London & North Eastern Railway.

Ambulance train

A specialist train was built at the York Carriage & Wagon Works in 1917, consisting of sixteen carriages which would become known officially as 'Continental Ambulance Train Number 37'. The ambulance train was one of many built during the First World War by the British railway companies, and were used for conveying injured soldiers to base hospitals both abroad and within Britain. The North Eastern Railway's ambulance train consisted of:

One Brake and Infectious Lying-down Car, carrying one of two train guards and eighteen lying-down 'cases' (the term used for the injured). This vehicle consisted of the brake compartment with hand brakes for stopping the train, as well as other miscellany which the brake compartment of any typical passenger train would have, with the addition of a living room for the guard. The infectious patients part of the carriage was divided into two sections for separating those with different kinds of infection, each section having a lavatory, sink and own water supply to prevent cross-infection. The two sections were not completely sealed – the only thing keeping them apart was a washable linen curtain. One section contained six cots, and the other section had twelve cots, separated into two compartments by a sliding door.

One Staff Car for the officers, carrying four Medical Officers, who would be members of the Royal Army Medical Corps, and four nurses, who would be members of the British Red Cross. One end of this carriage had a Mess Room for the RAMC Officers, with dining table, chairs and cupboard, and a lounge (which could be slid forward to make the seat an extra bed), with a similar Mess Room for the nurses at the other end of the carriage. There were also bedrooms on this carriage – three for the officers and two for the nurses, although one of the nurses' bedrooms had two beds, one above the other. Being for more senior members of staff, the carriage was well fitted out, with all bedrooms having wardrobe, table, chair, net racks, bookshelf and a radiator (the entire train was steam heated). Only the nurses had a lavatory on this carriage which included a shower and hot and cold water, the officers' lavatory being in the adjacent Kitchen Car. As the staff of the train would usually live on board even when a steam locomotive was not connected, *i.e.* awaiting to be loaded or for the next movement orders to come in, the Staff Car had a stove and hot water system for when the steam heating was not in use.

One Kitchen Car with accommodation for sitting sick officers carrying three cooks and accommodation for twenty cases. The large kitchen was fitted with an 'Army Dixie Range' (a 'Dixie' being a large cooking pot which could also be fitted with a lid for carrying) which would burn coal, coke or anthracite depending on what was available, a copper boiler and hot water installation with hot water tank above the stove, racks and cupboards, and two sinks with hot and cold water. The cooks lived in a single room with three beds tiered above each other, a falling table and a seat. As well as the aforementioned officers' lavatory there was also a pantry for the adjacent Officers' Staff Car. The rest of the carriage was for comfortable accommodation for twenty sick officers, who naturally would get superior accommodation to that of the lower ranks, which included seats on either side of the carriage facing inwards, with a table running down the centre, and net racks and book shelves, with adjacent lavatory.

Eight Ward Cars – separated into 1 Sick Officers' Lying-down Ward Car, 3 Ordinary Lying-down Ward Cars and 4 Ordinary Ward Cars. Despite the different designations for these cars, they were all fitted with 36 beds, or 'cots' as they are described, for lying-down cases arranged in three tiers, and in two rows, one on each side of the carriage, split in half by the space needed for the large double doors in the centre of the carriage on each side. Although designed for those required to lie down, the beds could be modified for those well enough to sit-up to increase capacity:

> Owing to the variation in the cases received for transfer to the Hospital Base the cots have been designed so that the centre tier may be hinged down to form a back to allow of the bottom cots being used as seats; this gives accommodation for 48 sitting cases, and as at the same time the top tier may be used for lying-down cases, the accommodation Is thus augmented to 60 cases.

To safeguard against patients falling out of the beds while the train was in motion, two leather straps were fitted to each bed – these ran down from the roof to the floor attached to each bed on the way. Each bed had a mattress filled with wood fibre (but described as 'comfortable') and two pillows filled with white flock. Each bed also had an ash tray, oddment rack and spitting cup bracket in convenient positions for the patient. Each Ward Car had a lavatory at one end, and a sink and cupboard provided at the other end.

One Pharmacy Car, placed in the centre of the Ward Cars for convenience, with five compartments. The first compartment was a Dispensary for medicines and fitted with cupboards, shelves, folding table, a hot water heater and a sink. The second was a Treatment Room with operating table, portable electric lamp and sterilizing facility. This is not an Americanisation as 'sterilizing' appears in the official booklet regarding the Ambulance Train. This room also had a large door opening to 8 feet 2 inches to allow a Standard Army Stretcher to be brought in. There was a minimum gangway between the Ward Cars and the Treatment Room of 2 feet 4 inches to allow a stretcher patient to be transported from anywhere they may be – as train had a gangway between each carriage for access. The third room was an Office with table, chairs, cupboards *etc.*; fourth, a Linen Room for bedding and other linen items, and fifth, a Pantry (for 'Medical Comforts').

One Infectious Sitting Car with capacity for 56 sitting-up cases and fourteen lying-down cases, split into seven compartments entered from a side corridor (or exterior side doors), again with a clearance of 2 feet 4 inches for stretchers, with each compartment having an upper cot for lying-down patients (with leather cushion filled with wood fibre), and the seating for sitting-up cases being made of wood and un-upholstered for hygiene purposes. Three of the compartments were "specially fitted for Mental Cases, iron bars being placed over the windows, and a swing door in the corridor to isolate this portion from the rest of the car". The carriage also had a lavatory with sink at one end and pantry at the other end.

One Kitchen and Mess Room Car for three cooks, with kitchen and living room/bedroom for the cooks similar to that in the Kitchen Car, but instead of officers' accommodation having two Mess Rooms, one for non-commissioned officers (such as Corporals and Sergeants) and one for 'men', these being the privates or other lower ranks in that unit (such as Air Mechanic in the Royal Flying Corps or Gunner in the Royal Field Artillery)

One Personnel Car with capacity for 33 Medical Orderlies, fitted out similarly to the Ward Cars but, as it was used for accommodation of the train personnel, extra room being allocated for shelving hence three less beds. There were also drawers under the lower beds of the three tiers of beds. This carriage could be used for patients if needed.

One Brake and Stores Car, again with one guard and necessary brake compartment and guard's living room, and the rest of the carriage having three store rooms (well secured with locks and keys) and a well-ventilated Meat Safe, with electric fan and chopping board.

In total the Ambulance Train could carry 445, but the bottom beds in the Ward Cars could also be used for seating sitting cases, in which case the accommodation could go up to 659. Good ventilation, cleanliness and light was a high priority in Hospitals and Ambulance Trains, with a large number of electric fans being placed along the train (with extra portable fans for gassed patients) and electric lighting and ventilators used. To aid with cleaning, rounded corners were used throughout the train and cemented floors were set in the lavatories, wash closets and treatment room in the Ward Car, elsewhere the flooring was covered in linoleum with the exception of kitchen floors in lead. Passenger comfort was thought of too – travelling for an injured patient could be agony, often unavoidable in motor and horse-drawn ambulances travelling over poor roads, but Ambulance Trains were made as smooth riding as possible – the North Eastern Railway's Ambulance Train having bolster, side bearing and auxiliary springs on the four-wheeled bogies which carried each carriage, and fitted with 'patent cushioned wheels'.

Ambulance Train 37 measured 890 feet and 8 inches in total, and weighed around 465 tons when fully loaded (without a locomotive). As with all Ambulance Trains, it was painted in khaki overall, with the Geneva Red Cross on a white background approximately halfway along each carriage on both sides, painted over the window panels and frames. It was one of 43 British Ambulance Trains that worked abroad – most on the western front, but at least three served in Italy and one in Egypt. At least twenty-two further Ambulance Trains were used in the UK, and nineteen were built, or converted, for use by the American Expeditionary Force, including one built by the North Eastern Railway identical to Ambulance Train 37, but had not left York by the time the Armistice was signed and so was not needed, and most likely converted for passenger use. Before going to the Continent, Ambulance Train 37 was used as an exhibit for the general public to raise funds for the British Red Cross, with 36,404 people taking the opportunity to tour the train and raising £1,802, 5s 10d. A special booklet was also produced with description, drawings and photographs of the Ambulance Train, the front cover showing a Raven 'Atlantic' Express engine on the front. Although the Ambulance Train did not start its work in Europe until the second half of 1917, it still rendered valuable assistance to the medical evacuation of the injured to large Base Hospitals or back to Britain.

Train control centre

A new train control centre was inaugurated on 3 December 1917 – the Tyneside Freight Train Control, located in Newcastle in a large room next to the Divisional Superintendent's Freight Train Office. This 'control' covered an area from Benton Bank Box in the north, Ouston Junction to the south, Heaton and Park Lane Yards in the east and Blaydon in the west. The concept itself was not new, as a similar control had been in use since 14 November 1910 at Middlesbrough covering the Newport–Middlesbrough area, but this new control had some differences. The control worked by using telephone connections with signal boxes and traffic offices so that passage of freight trains was reported to the control and replicated on a large control board, being run by three chief controllers working in alternate shifts, with assistants, and all supervised by W. Powney, Chief Freight Train Clerk. As well as simply the location of each train, at the control office the number and class of engine was known, the make-up and load of the train (for example, a pink ticket represented an Admiralty coal train, and a white ticket with diagonal red line represented a special goods train, whereas a white one was a booked goods train, *etc.*), and the origin and destination of the train. It did not quite go as far as knowing the names of the crew, but it did also show the times they signed on for work and so how long they could be expected to work for. The control was very successful in keeping the busy railways in the Tyneside area flowing as best as possible, and with 151 separate points of telephone communication in the control's area, any delays or problems could be diagnosed and dealt with as soon as possible.

Wartime demands

As an extreme example of the short notice demands placed on the railways during wartime, in December the North Eastern Railway was asked to store 50,000 sinkers, for use with sea mines, coming in from manufacturers around the country, until they could be put in the sea complete with accompanying mine. They were stored at Darlington, West Hartlepool and Scarborough, and as well as being simply handled and stored were also subjected to examination when they arrived in stores. Checks made on their condition, sending reports to the Admiralty how many arrived, and where, each week, and they could only be removed from stores with a warrant from the Admiralty. The following excerpt details the massive logistical headache of how they were organised and stored:

At Darlington the sinkers were stored in a paint shop attached to the N.E.R. Loco. Works (Stooperdale). The first of them were received in December, 1917, and the last were dispatched in March, 1919. The total number handled during that period was 13,420. The sinkers weighed, approximately, 8 cwts each. They were at first slung up by means of a steam travelling-crane and lifted out of the wagons direct on to the stack; but as the stack grew in size it was found necessary to take the sinkers out of the wagons before entering the shop and they were then transported along a temporary run-way, known as "Jerusalem rails".

At West Hartlepool accommodation was afforded for 13,000 sinkers, space being reserved on the ground floors of two warehouses and on the first and second floors of one of the warehouses. The sinkers began to arrive in December, 1917, and the stock was finally cleared in February, 1920. During this period a total of 14,233 sinkers were dealt with. The largest number on hand at one time was 13,187. Special gear on the block and tackle principle had to be installed for stacking on the ground floors. The difficulty of stacking on the upper floors was overcome by the erection of outside platforms on each floor and the use of the dockside electric cranes for lifting. Portable rails were fixed between these temporary stages and the stacks.

At Scarborough, passenger traffic was very light during the war period, and it was found possible to use the cab-stand and one of the platforms for storage. The sinkers began to arrive at the end of January, 1918, and were dealt with by a gang of seven men. By the middle of June, 1918, there had been received 5,132 sinkers, and these, it was found, took up all the available space. Use was made of 462 wagons to convey the sinkers to Scarborough. None of the sinkers were removed during the war, but on 24 March 1919, the Admiralty ordered their removal to depots, the last being dispatched on 29 May. For the purpose of stacking, a special swivel crane had to be 'rigged up'

Derailment

On 19 December, as the Up East Coast express train from Edinburgh to London King's Cross was passing through Alne station at a speed of around fifty-five mph, the couplings between the second and third, and third and fourth vehicles on the train became divided following an initial derailment. The locomotive and first two vehicles carried forward and came to rest with a gap of around half-a-mile between the front portion and the third portion. The locomotive was a North Eastern Railway 4-4-2 'Atlantic' locomotive driven by C. Wilkinson and fired by T. S. Johnson. The first they became aware of an issue with the train was when they felt a check to the engine's speed "as if there had been an application of the brake due to the communication cord having been operated"; they also noticed a drop in brake vacuum pressure and so shut off steam. The pressure gauge had by now dropped to zero, and so realising this meant the train had become detached looked behind and noticed only two vehicles attached behind the locomotive, and the second one was oscillating. With the brake now fully applied the locomotive and two carriages came to a stop, as did the two detached portions of the train as the brakes were automatically applied following loss of vacuum.

It transpired that the rearmost axle and pair of wheels on the rear bogie of the second vehicle had become derailed when the axle snapped exactly in the middle. At first the axle fracture did not cause any major issues until the communication cord was pulled, probably by a passenger realising something was untoward in the running of the carriage. This had the effect of applying the brakes of the train and made the two halves of the axle fall from the bogie and caused serious damage to the permanent way. It also fouled the undersides of the third and following vehicles. One half of the axle with its one wheel was found under the fifth vehicle, and the other half near the rear of the fourteenth vehicle, three vehicles from the rear of the train. The damage from this is the likely cause of the breaking of the couplings between the third and fourth vehicles, the 'clean' break between the second and third vehicles apparently occurring slightly later when the coupling of the second vehicle, now riding lower at the rear owing to the missing axle and wheels, simply dropped below the coupling on the third vehicle, unfastening the coupling.

The second vehicle was an East Coast Joint Stock carriage built by the North Eastern Railway at York in 1898 but re-axled in 1913. The carriage had undergone a repair and thorough overhaul in July 1917 just a few months before the derailment, and the axles and wheels would have been examined as part of the overhaul. Another axle from the same batch of fifty as the defective axle was found and put under stringent tests to see if any flaw could be detected, but the axle passed the tests and there were no indications of any flaw in the production of the axle or in the quality of the material used. The broken axle was thoroughly inspected, and the only possible flaw that could be found was slight evidence of pitting three-quarters of an inch inside the axle, which possibly indicated a flaw there, and this was regarded as the "most probably cause of the failure of the axle and of the subsequent derailment"

1918 and Beyond

1918 was to be the final year of the war against Germany, but it was not obvious to those fighting at the time. After the Russians left the war in 1917, German soldiers from the Eastern Front were released to fight on the Western Front, commencing with Operation Michael on 21 March 1918. The Germans, aided by poor visibility and using storm trooper tactics, ignored pockets of resistance and aimed for deep penetration of the British and French lines, making great advances before stretching their lines of supply to breaking point until the advance was checked. The stalemate of the Western Front was now broken, and from the Battle of Amiens in August onwards the British, French and now Americans were continually on the offensive, pushing the Germans back until the armistice was signed on 11 November. This was preceded by Bulgaria on 29 September, the Ottoman Empire on 30 October and Austria-Hungary on 5 November. Despite the end of hostilities, there was still the chance of war resuming until the Treaty of Versailles was signed on 28 June 1919. Fighting was still happening in Russia where the British and French aided the White forces in trying to defeat the Communist Red forces, but all to no avail.

In the United Kingdom, on 6 February, the Representation of the People Act gave women over the age of thirty (as long as they were a householder or married to a householder) the right to vote, and extended the vote to male householders over the age of 21.

Food wastage and rationing

The effects of submarine warfare and the war in general after several years meant thoughts were turning to rationing – Sir Arthur Yapp introduced a voluntary ration scheme in early 1918, whereby each participant would sign a voluntary pledge and stick to the guidelines to ensure no food was wasted, and this would hopefully avoid the need for compulsory rationing. The scheme took into account the extra dietary requirements of manual workers, which of course would include many railway workers vital to the war effort. The name of this scheme was the 'League of National Safety'.

An enquiry was held in early 1918 by the Ministry of Food to discuss the problem of food wastage whilst in the care of railway or shipping companies – from loss during handling or rain to contamination by other cargoes. The North Eastern Railway was fully aware of this and special care was taught to all employees who handled goods, but it was impressed again upon staff that they should take care, especially in light of potential food shortages;

> A faulty sheet, for instance, may ruin more grain than could be grown on a large field, lack of protection against frost will waste the produce of a dozen allotments; negligence in putting bacon, cheese, tea, sugar or indeed any foodstuffs in contact with oils, corrosive liquids or smelly merchandise, or traces of these on wagon bottoms may ruin a shop's supplies and cause many to go hungry. It is no longer a matter of money only, but of National Safety.

Rationing came into effect in early 1918 to try and ensure that food shortages would not happen – it was nowhere near as severe as in the Second World War, however. Sugar, butter and margarine were first to be rationed, later followed by meat and cheese – the rationing required that each member of the public be registered to a certain supplier of these goods and so that supplier would be allotted a certain amount. Germany on the other hand was suffering severely owing to the Royal Navy's blockade of German ports, and malnourishment was a serious issue.

Railwaymen visit the front

Thirteen North Eastern Railway men visited the Western Front in March, as part of a party of 350 railwaymen following an invitation from the Government via the National Union of Railwaymen. This was no mere sight-seeing trip, and the dangers they faced were made all too apparent when the party's first port of call upon arrival in France was to a 'gas school', where they were trained on how to use the Small Box Respirator, the standard gas mask used by the British Army from late 1916 onwards. After their instruction, they were then put in a gas chamber where they would put their instruction to use, the chamber being filled with gas necessitating the use of the equipment. The next day the men were shown a food and forage depot, where the irony of using German built electric cranes was not lost on the men, one of whom, Signalman F. W. Topping of Walkergate, reported on the trip in the *North Eastern Railway Magazine*.

On the third day of the visit, a train journey was made further inland, giving the men an appreciation of the work done by the Railway Operating Division, but also remarking that 'there was no fear of the axles becoming heated', alluding to the slow pace of railway journeys on the Western Front. Upon arriving at the destination station the men got into motor cars and drove closer to the front, starting to pass towns in further and further states of destruction, arriving at Albert where the golden Madonna on top of the Basilica, due to shell damage, was perched at right angles to its original position. Many French and British believed that the war would end when the statue finally fell, and ironically it was the British who finally knocked it off when the Germans took Albert during the later German spring offensive of 1918, as it was thought the tower would be used as a German observation post. The men then got back into the motor cars and headed to a Tank base where they were repaired, and had the chance to see a Tank being put through its paces on a prepared fake battlefield. After this they headed to a real battlefield and got to see what the conditions were like there, seeing field graves of men found and recorded by the Graves Registration Department, and also seeing the results of a mine blown up under the German front line, the resulting crater resembling a "big chalk quarry". The tour continued further behind what was the German lines, seeing the trail of destruction left after the Battle of the Somme as the Germans retreated to the prepared Hindenburg Line. The next day they were shown the remains of a 'famous city' previously held by the Germans, seeing the underground tunnels which included a complete hospital with operating theatre and wards. Next the men walked across "a ridge famous in the history of the war" – most likely Vimy Ridge, captured by the Canadians in 1917 – "the effects of the bombardment were more visible than ever; not an inch of ground was there which had not been turned up". The next day a large repair factory was visited, the size of which bewildered the men – amongst other items, 11,400 pairs of boots were repaired a day, 900 wheels, 1,600 tins and 2,000 dixies (used for cooking) were repaired a week, all by German prisoners of war. Around 1,400 helmets were painted by French girls, two to each helmet, one to paint and the other to camouflage and put sand on them to stop them reflecting the sun and giving away their position. 11,000 rifles, 11,000 bayonets and 50 machine guns were also repaired there a week. Any items sent there for repair that were found to be beyond use had parts salvaged where possible (ie the upper leather parts of boots for boot laces or damaged tents made into horse feed bags). The time taken to inspect the factory took so long that there was no time to visit a nearby hospital and aerodrome as planned. The men all returned with a further profound respect for the men of the armed forces, not just the army but also the Royal Navy who were engaged in the safe transportation of men, women, animals, machines and munitions across the English Channel. Despite the news of the German spring offensive which broke not long after their return, the correspondent was certain there was nothing to fear despite the dark days ahead, owing to the strength of the armed forces.

Death at Marsh Lane

At Marsh Lane station in Leeds on 11 March, long serving member of staff J. E. Lennox suffered a seizure and died whilst on duty, collecting tickets. Lennox had served on the North Eastern Railway since 8 June 1874, initially as a signalman at Sherburn and various other points on the railway until his appointment as a ticket collector in August 1898. He was well known in his local community for his interests in music and religious duties, including a spell as the conductor of a male voice choir in Leeds.

Caring for those left behind

For some time, the North Eastern Railway had employed staff to visit the families and dependents of soldiers and sailors who were formerly members of North Eastern Railway staff, especially with regards to payments to them from the North Eastern Railway to supplement a man's pay. The role of the visitors was to ascertain any change of circumstances in the man or his dependents, any promotions or reductions in rank and the dates on which they took effect which would affect the man's pay, any alterations in the number of dependents and any child dependents reaching sixteen years of age – at this age, Government Allowance for them then stopped.

They also asked about any cases of hardship, and whether the man was wounded at all. In the case of a man being killed in action, missing in action or dying on service, it was also requested that a photograph of them should be obtained for use in the *North Eastern Railway Magazine* Roll of Honour. By May 1918 there were nine members of staff, all female, undertaking this role – three at Hull and one each at Leeds, Gateshead, Darlington, Newcastle, Sunderland and West Hartlepool, with enquiries being made as to whether they would be of use at York also.

One case was recorded on 28 May 1918 of a married man who had left North Eastern Railway service and enlisted without permission, which meant he was not eligible for an allowance from the railway. He was sadly killed in action, leaving a widow and four children, and in light of their circumstances, and despite him enlisting without permission, they were given a grant of money from the North Eastern Railway Relief Fund. Another case was that of a widow who was recommended the allowance but was instead found employment at Shildon and the allowance was stopped as she was now in paid work.

An unusual meeting

On 15 March an unusual meeting between a civilian and a German prisoner of war was noticed by a station master at an unidentified North Eastern Railway station. A train of German prisoners of war drew into the station near where a number of British civilians, men discharged from military service in plain clothing, were standing. As a German officer doctor got off the train, he and one of the civilians recognised each other immediately. It transpired that the man was formerly a Sergeant in France when his part of the lines was overrun by the Germans. The Sergeant received a bullet wound, and the doctor was tending to his injury when the British counter-attacked and drove the Germans back.

New works

By 1918 the additional demands on the North Eastern Railway network required more lines to be laid down, as well as having lines removed elsewhere to be sent to the front for military railways on the Western Front. Between Newcastle and Berwick and Newcastle and Carlisle additional running lines had been built – for example between Newcastle and Berwick, there was nearly double the traffic being run on the lines in early 1918 than there had been in 1913, and over double between Newcastle and Carlisle. With coal being ran across the system rather than direct to ports and shipped from there, this also required extra sidings and running lines to be built, with coal from the Durham coalfield heading to London, the Midlands and West Cumberland. In order that the coal trains could be staged from the Durham area southwards, additional sidings were added at Darlington and three groups of sidings were built at York. Munitions works in Newcastle and shipbuilding on the north-east coast also required extra trains, and related to these were new marshalling sidings at Heaton. Minor works were also common, often sidings at various stations, notably for the handling of home-grown timber.

The war also meant the cancellation of some passenger services, such as the 12.20 Newcastle to Sheffield express which was marketed as "the fastest train in the British Empire" – the straight and well-engineered stretch of 44½ miles between Darlington and York covered in a scheduled time of 43 minutes, equalling 61.57 mph.

Tank on tour

24 March saw a metal beast photographed in Darlington on a North Eastern Railway 40-ton quintuple bolster wagon – a Mk IV 'Male' Tank named 'Egbert'. 'Egbert' was one of six 'Tank Banks' that toured Britain from late 1917 up until the end of the war to sell war bonds and war savings certificates, using the huge interest from the general public in the Tanks, especially following the successful mass use of them at the Battle of Cambrai in November 1917. Two Tanks took part in the Lord Mayor's Show in November 1917, and from 26 November 'Egbert', showing battle scars, likely from the Third Battle of Ypres rather than Cambrai which only started on 20 November (although interestingly was without the rails on top of the Tank for un-ditching apparatus which all Mk IVs in action received), was put on display in Trafalgar Square. Afterwards, 'Egbert' and five other Male Tanks toured the country as 'Tank Banks', being the subject of much publicity, with Royal Flying Corps aeroplanes dropping leaflets announcing the visit in advance, and its arrival accompanied by bands, speeches, soldiers, celebrities and local dignitaries. The amount raised for the war effort was reported in the press to encourage local competition, and it was announced that 'Egbert' would be donated after the war to the town that raised the most – the eventual winner being West Hartlepool. Although Tanks were needed at the front, the monies raised by these six tanks far outweighed any other use they were put to, and were a sign of the need for more money as the war entered its fourth year, in which more men were to die than any other year of the war.

Derailment

On 15 April a derailment occurred between Newby Wiske and Sinderby stations in North Yorkshire to the 11.25 a.m. Northallerton to Leeds express, pulled by 4-4-0 No. 1244, an R1 Class engine of

1909. When travelling between the two stations, the tender and all the coaches came off the rails, and the train split between the second and third coaches – eventually coming to rest with 110 yards between the two portions. The accident was first noticed when the engine driver, Mr Falkingham, noticed the tender rocking when there had been no previous unusual movement to it. Quickly realising that this meant that the tender had come off the railway he shut the regulator and applied the brake, only realising the train had divided once he came to a stop and left the engine. The accident was fortunate in that the tender and first two derailed coaches were, at the time they came off the rails, travelling over a bridge carrying the railway over the River Swale, but fortunately they stayed vertical on the ballast and were not at risk of falling into the river below which would have had disastrous consequences. Two passengers received minor injuries, and the vehicles involved in the derailment received serious damage – axle boxes were broken, glass smashed, and panelling, steps, truss rods, hose pipes etc were also damaged, as well as 300 yards of the railway being completely destroyed. As well as the possibility of coaches coming off the River Swale bridge, a small fire started underneath one of the coaches which was gas lit, caused by a fracture in a gas regulator, and the escaping gas was ignited, likely to have been caused by sparks during the derailment from the wheels and frame of the bogie in which they sat. As soon as the fire was noticed by North Eastern Railway Gateman by the name of Kilvington, he immediately threw out all cushions and rugs from the carriage and then went to get two fire extinguishers from the brake compartment of the carriage. Two soldiers, Private J. Nicholson of 360th Employment Company and Private R. J. Hollis of the 15th Battalion South Lancashire Regiment used the fire extinguishers, stopping it from spreading. The quick actions of these three men stopped the fire from gaining hold of the wooden carriages. Only one of the nine carriages in the train was electrically lit, showing that despite the tragic death toll of the Quintinshill rail disaster, not all carriages had been converted to electric lighting.

Despite investigation the cause of the accident was not decided – the tender was the first vehicle of the train to become derailed, but on the rails where the derailment is likely to have occurred there were gouge marks which were caused by a heavier wheel than those used on a carriage or tender, however close inspection of the large wheels on the locomotive found no damage nor any damage or missing parts anywhere on the locomotive.

Fire at Walkergate

Serious damaged was caused to the North Eastern Railway's electrified suburban passenger services in the North Tyneside area when a large fire destroyed the carriage sheds at Walkergate on 11 August, and thirty-four carriages of the electric multiple units employed on these services were either wrecked or severely damaged. In the meantime, steam-hauled passenger services had to supplement the electric multiple units still available, until an all-electric service was restored on 12 September. The damaged electric units would not be replaced until the 1920s when replacements, with elliptical roofs rather than the original clerestories, were built at York, as well as a replacement carriage shed.

More women needed

The need for more women to join the war effort was increasing by 1918 – although women were filling the men's jobs at home, as the war went on women were needed to join military services to release men in non-combatant roles for front line duties. A public meeting to persuade women to join the services was made in Darlington on 12 October, which culminated in a procession of members of the Queen Mary's Army Auxiliary Corps (originally named the Women's Army Auxiliary Corps, but changed to the QMAAC in 1918), Women's Royal Air Force and Women's Royal Naval Service, as well as munitions workers, each band of women headed by their own banner. The munitions workers from the Darlington 'shell shop' were of course there in quantity, and to go with their display they had a specially decorated North Eastern Railway horse-drawn trailer, tastefully decorated with images of King George V and Queen Mary, and also various shells as produced at the factory.

Armistice

The signing of the armistice on 11 November 1918, which resulted in the end of hostilities on the Western Front, was marked with celebration around the country. In the Darlington drawing register, George Heppell, Chief Draughtsman, made a simple entry for 11 November – with '11.00 a.m.' under the Diagram Number heading, the description was "ARMISTICE SIGNED". After more than four years of war great change had occurred on the North Eastern Railway. Not only had men gone away and women come in to fill their places, but there were the effects of austerity and of the huge demands made in supplying the needs of the armed forces. Furthermore, the railway itself had come under attack from the enemy on several occasions. The December 1918 edition of the *North Eastern Railway Magazine* opened with the Roll of Honour, with the words "It is with deep sorrow that in the hour of victory we have to record the names of nearly 100 more NER men who had given their lives towards victory before the signing of the Armistice on November 11, 1918. This gives the high total of 1,745 men killed since 1914, or approximately 10 per cent of the number to enlisted".

Allotments

At the end of the war, John Howe who compiled and wrote many articles on allotments for the *North Eastern Railway Magazine* (as detailed in the '1917' chapter) wrote the following the lines for the magazine stressing the continued importance of the humble allotment;

> Even though the dawn of peace is upon us, it is still the duty of each allottee to produce as much foodstuff as possible. There will still be a scarcity of food for a few year years throughout the world.

John Howe died on 9 December 1918, and even up to the last few hours of his life he had been revising a booklet called "The Allotment Year". He had died of influenza at the age of 52. The 'Spanish Flu' killed between 50-100 million people (between 3 and 5 per cent of the world's population at the time), a truly global pandemic that was helped to spread by soldiers returning at the end of the war.

Repatriated prisoners of war

Now the war was over, the thousands of prisoners taken by Germany were to be brought home as soon as possible, following little or no contact with their loved ones since entering captivity. Sunday 18 November saw the first shipload of repatriated prisoners land at Hull aboard the SS *Archangel*, and from then between 2,500 and 3,000 prisoners returned back to the UK daily via Hull, and the reception they received was just as warm on the days following the first batch. When the men left the ship, the first port of call were canteens run by the Army and Navy Canteen Board where they were welcomed back with tea, coffee and other food and refreshments, and then handed a parcel of food, tobacco, cigarettes and a pipe. They were also given postcards with which to write to loved ones to let them know of their arrival in the UK, and then posted as soon as possible. With each arrival of ex-prisoner ships the North Eastern Railway put on six or seven special trains a day to Ripon from where onwards they were processed.

Demobilisation

Now the war was over, the majority of troops were eager to return home, but the logistics of this were enormous and it did not go as quickly or smoothly as hoped – the Government turned to the North Eastern Railway for help once again and Sir Eric Campbell Geddes, who at the time was First Lord of the Admiralty, was put in charge of the 'Co-ordination of Demobilisation Section of the War Cabinet'.

As the men returned home, those fit and able returned to their jobs, and the women who had done such vital work for the North Eastern Railway left the railway. Unfortunately not all of those that returned were fit or able, but where possible the North Eastern Railway found light work for five hundred injured men that returned, setting up a departmental committee with two sympathetic inspectors to find work for them on the system – at the same time they looked after the well-being of those members of staff who required special treatment for their injuries.

A scheme was also set up whereby the Traffic Apprentices Training Committee reviewed cases of men who before the war were in low grade roles, but during the war had distinguished themselves in their conduct, especially those that had risen through the ranks to become commissioned officers.

One man who tried to use his wartime experience to find re-employment on the North Eastern Railway was not so lucky – Jon Thomas Bennett's father wrote to the North Eastern Railway in February 1920, his father was an engine driver at Edinburgh saying that despite issues which caused him to cease to be employed by the North Eastern Railway before his wartime service, his service to his country had proved his worth and requested he be re-employed by the railway, saying he was young and foolish before the termination of his employment and his military service made him more mature. This was followed up two weeks later by a letter from Bennett himself re-iterating what his father said and further explaining how his wartime service in France and Belgium made him a suitable candidate for re-employment with the railway. Enquiries were made into Bennett, and it was found that he used to be a fireman on the railway at Edinburgh – on 3 December 1915 he came into work drunk when he was supposed to be on duty for relief work at Edinburgh shed, bawling and shouting when he came into the office and saying he would quit and wreck the office if fines for previous offences were not refunded to him. Two North British Railway Policemen had to come to take him away and he was sacked from North Eastern Railway service.

One former colleague of his provided a letter to support this;

> This man Bennett may pretend to feel his position but I think there is no doubt about it that he is very intemperate, insolent and lazy, and cannot be relied upon to come to work. More worthy can be employed.

Eventually his request was turned down personally in writing by Chief Mechanical Engineer Raven on 7 January 1921.

New Chief of North Eastern Railway Police

In 1919, E. T. Barrel was made the new Chief of the North Eastern Railway Police. He had been the acting Chief since the outbreak of war, as the previous Chief was made General Horwood, Provost Marshal of British Forces in France. After the war he went to the Metropolitan Police Force as Assistant Commissioner. Barrel had not had an easy time during the war – exactly half of the North Eastern Railway policemen were spared for service with the armed forces and promptly enlisted. By 1917 women had started to be sworn in to fill the gaps. Of the North Eastern Railway Policemen that enlisted, three became commissioned officers, eleven were killed, nine commemorated for their actions, and four became prisoners, two of them during the Mons Retreat in 1914. Many more were wounded.

The last roll of honour was published in the January 1920 edition of the *North Eastern Railway Magazine*, with five men honoured.

The North Eastern Railway itself was to last until 1923, still under the control of the Railway Executive Committee, when most of the railways in Britain were grouped into four main railways following the Railways Act of 1921 – the North Eastern Railway was grouped with, amongst others, the Great Northern Railway, North British Railway, Great Eastern Railway and Great Central Railway to create the London & North Eastern Railway, coming into effect on 1 January 1923.

Remembering

It has often occurred to me that something should be undertaken to perpetuate the memory of so many of our gallant friends and colleagues from the N.E.R. who have made the great sacrifice for freedom. The war being virtually over I consider the time opportune for making this suggestion. 1,745 is the sad total shown in the current issue of our Magazine, in killed alone. A small sum subscribed by each of the employees on our vast system would, I think, realise sufficient to erect a fitting tribute to our lost fellow-workers. How about a memorial placed at a good centre like York?

Mr F. Ascough, Traffic Foreman, Hartlepool, late 1918

With the signing of the Armistice and cessation of hostilities on the Western Front on 11 November 1918, the war was effectively over, although the war did not officially end until the signing of the Treaty of Versailles on 28 June 1919. All over the country people wanted to create lasting memorials to the men and women who had died in the service of their country. As well as the graves of men on the battlefields, and large memorials such as at Thiepval on the Somme and the Menin Gate in Ypres which listed those killed with no known grave, memorials were built in villages, towns and cities in prominent public places to remember their dead. Often they would list all the names of those killed from that area, although in larger populaces such as cities this was not always possible, and places of work, schools, universities *etc.* often had plaques recording those who had left those places to serve and not return.

A review undertaken at the end of 1917 gave the total of dead or missing from the North Eastern Railway (not including those killed whilst still employed by the North Eastern Railway such as those killed in the East Coast bombardment or 1916 Zeppelin raid on York) as 1,133. As mentioned in the quotation above, taken from a letter published in the *North Eastern Railway Magazine* in late 1918, by the end of 1918 this figure stood at 1,745. Understandably the NER was proud of these men, many who had served with the North Eastern Railway Battalion, and joined the many other companies in commemorating their dead. On 10 May 1919 four separate services were held at York Minster, Newcastle Cathedral, Holy Trinity Church in Hull and St Mary's Church in Gateshead, in honour of the NER men killed – by then known to exceed 2,000 with the figure rising, mainly as men declared missing were now officially presumed dead. Relatives of the dead received individual invitations to attend and all NER staff were given admission if requested. To cope with demand, ordinary services were strengthened and special trains were put on. York, as headquarters of the company, was understandably the busiest, and the Minster was packed with 6,000 members of the congregation and the other three services were also struggling with large numbers.

At Gateshead, the Rector, Reverend H. S. Stephenson, composed several verses for the occasion;

In Memoriam
Dear comrades of the N.E.R.
From shop and office, yard and brake,
You ran on time to fields of War
And kept the rails for England's sake.

We trusted you in days of peace,
Brave guardians of our iron way,
We knew in war beyond the seas
You'd hear the signal "Right away."

You simply drove on straight ahead,
And watched the Bright and Morning Star;
For you no danger lamp shone red,
And yet you did not travel far.

You kept the footplate to the last;
That was the reason why you'd come.
Your Chief is calling: Time is past;
Lo, yonder signal is "The Home."

Eventually the final total of men from the North Eastern Railway killed during the war came to 2,236. With the figure finalised, work could begin on a permanent memorial. Sir Edwin Lutyens was commissioned by the company to build the memorial, who already had prior form for memorials as before the war had even ended he was made one of the three main architects for the Imperial War Graves Commission and had designed many monuments – the most famous being The Cenotaph in Whitehall, London. The site chosen for the memorial was adjacent to the company's 1906-built head office in York, just inside the medieval City walls, on land which was formerly the original York station's coal depot and carriage sidings. Work started in 1923 and when the memorial was unveiled, the North Eastern Railway had ceased to exist following the amalgamation into the London North Eastern Railway.

The unveiling of the memorial took place on 14 June 1924 by Field Marshal Lord Plumer in front of a crowd of between 5,000 and 6,000 people. Dignitaries present included the Lord Mayors of York, Bradford and Hull, the Sheriff of York, Chief General Manager Ralph Wedgwood and other Officers of the London & North Eastern Railway, and also the former Directors of the North Eastern Railway and current Directors of the London & North Eastern Railway. Sentries with arms reversed were posted at the four corners of the central stone of remembrance, supplied by the 1st Battalion Durham Light Infantry, with Trumpeters from the 8th King's Royal Irish Hussars. Following prayers led by the Lord Archbishop of York and Reverend Alfred Lee of Newcastle , Lord Plumer then unveiled the memorial, and after his address the Trumpeters sounded the Last Post, followed by the customary two minutes' silence to remember the dead. The memorial was built from Portland Stone, which following Sir Edward Lutyen's first use of it after the war became the standard material for memorials and Commonwealth War Grave Commission gravestones. The memorial consisted of an obelisk, with the North Eastern Railway company mark, in a wreath, at the base. Underneath is the inscription;

IN ABIDING
REMEMBRANCE
OF THE 2236 MEN
OF
THE NORTH EASTERN
RAILWAY
WHO GAVE
THEIR LIVES
FOR THEIR COUNTRY
IN THE GREAT WAR
THE COMPANY
PLACES
THIS MONUMENT

The walls which surround the memorial on three sides record the names of those men, with the Stone of Remembrance in the centre. Over the years since the unveiling, the names on the soft Portland Stone have in places eroded heavily. However, in November 2011 BRB (Residuary) Ltd, a residuary body who, as successor to the British Railways Board following the privatisation of British Rail, are responsible for non-operational railway land (amongst other roles such as pensions) unveiled new plaques on one of the side walls of the memorial designed and produced by the Railway Ex-Servicemen's Association which list the men's names again, but much more clarified. The large memorial, situated within the walls of York next to both the 1906 Head Office featuring beautiful Edwardian architecture, and the York Old Station, is a fitting and lasting reminder of the 2,236 who did not return.

On War Service

'We arrived in Portsmouth in fine style because at some point during the night we had to wait and all seven engines were coupled together. Seven 'Geordies' all in a line. What a photograph it would have made!'

Percy Rosewarne

As well as men leaving for service in the Army and Navy, locomotives, rolling stock and other North Eastern Railway property was to play its part in the war.

Motor vehicles

When the war started, the Army was in desperate need of transport to match the rapid expansion in manpower. The British Army had recognised the worth of motor vehicles in the years preceding the war, and a Subsidy scheme had been in place since 1911. The idea behind the Subsidy scheme was that a suitable lorry for War Office use could be bought from certain manufacturers (the main ones were Dennis, Thornycroft, AEC and Leyland), and the civilian owners would receive subsidy payments for owning the lorry on the condition that if it was needed such as in case of war, the vehicle would be given back to the War Office. As successful as this scheme was, still more were needed. Seventeen of the railway's most modern motor omnibuses and charabancs were thus requisitioned for War Office use in October 1914.

To be more precise, only the chassis (the term 'chassis' in this instance refers to a running chassis – engine, radiator, bonnet, driving equipment, wheels *etc.*, not just the metal frame) – conversions to lorries were made at York Carriage Works. The motor buses, a mixture of Maudslays and Leylands, less than a year old, along with four Leyland 40 hp charabancs of 1912 were fitted with new cabs and wooden lorry bodies, with the familiar WD (standing for War Department) with the broad 'crow's foot' arrow between the 'W' and the 'D' emblazoned on the side of the lorry body. The bus bodies were stored at York for future use – after the requisitioning of the chassis, the North Eastern Railway made an order for twelve replacement Leyland chassis, the order being authorised on 12 November 1914, but unsurprisingly they were not delivered until October and November 1919 when Leyland's war work was done. The completed seventeen requisitioned North Eastern Railway vehicles had their conversions finished at the same time – two photographs taken of the completed lorries in War Department specification lined up in Knavesmire, York shows at least five Maudslays, one of the 1914 built Leylands and two of the 1912 Leyland charabancs converted. One of these photographs was published in the December 1914 issue of the *North Eastern Railway Magazine*, showing the vehicles ready to leave York for Salisbury Plain. The note regarding the vehicles also mentions that sixteen drivers from the NER Motor Vehicle Department are already serving at the front – trained and experienced motor vehicle drivers being in much demand at the time by the Army.

The single Commer built motor vehicle owned by the company, a 1908 built example with an interchangeable flatbed lorry and van body, was also commandeered in 1914 but no other information is known about it – it seems rather surprising that they took a six year old vehicle when there were still more modern vehicles to choose from.

The loss of twelve of the Company's newest motor buses, as well as four of the most modern charabancs and a (albeit relatively elderly in NER motor vehicle terms) goods vehicle, was not quite as severe a loss as it may first seem – loss of manpower both from the Company and of the general population meant that there was less demand for passenger services, and they were almost completely suspended. At least twenty-four of the Company's charabancs (a large open-top vehicle fitted with five or six benches which rose up on three steps along the body, very popular before buses became common place and often used for tourist trips owing to the visibility offered to the occupants) were converted with goods bodies during the war for delivering parcels and cargo. Although originally delivered as charabancs, with interchangeable bus bodies for colder parts of the year, at least three of the charabancs, two 1910 Fiats and a 1908 Hallford, were delivered with interchangeable charabanc, bus and lorry bodies so it is likely their original lorry bodies were fitted and not newly fitted as such. The other charabancs were delivered with interchangeable charabanc and bus bodies – usually the charabanc bodies would be fitted during the summer months and the roofed bus bodies for the colder parts of the year.

Of the vehicles that remained in North Eastern Railway service during the war, aside from a drop in staffing levels, one problem faced was that of fuel. Petrol was of course in huge demand for military vehicles, as the British Army rapidly became more mechanised using not just motor lorries and staff cars, but also ambulances, artillery tractors and of course tanks and aeroplanes. The Royal Navy needed petrol for their aeroplanes, airships and small naval craft. One alternative was to convert vehicles to run on gas derived from coal, the gas kept in large inflated 'gas bags' on top of vehicles, with a wooden or metal framework in place to stop it drooping over the sides of the vehicle when empty. This method of keeping vehicles running during fuel shortages is most often associated with the Second World War, but was also a fairly common sight during the First World War. The sight of these gas-powered vehicles was very unusual and almost comical – the Chief Automobile Engineer of the General Post Office, Major C. Wheeler, mentioned them as 'large clumsy affairs which flopped about on the tops of hoods and canopies. We were much amused at the sight of these gadgets when visiting London.' A single photograph exists of one of the North Eastern Railway's three 1914 built Leyland single-deck omnibuses, registration BT1508, with a gas bag on the roof of the vehicle showing that at least one of the company's vehicles was converted to run on gas. Unfortunately it has not been possible to discover whether any other North Eastern Railway vehicles were converted to run on coal gas, or for how long they were powered in this way, however other motor bus operators around the country also used coal gas to power their vehicles as the war went on.

Although not requisitioned by the War Office, at least one of the North Eastern Railway's vans served the army – in the January 1915 edition of the *North Eastern Railway Magazine*, an article on the North Eastern Railway Battalion in billets on the east coast shows two civilian motor vehicles – one of them is a 1908 Hallford van belonging to the North Eastern Railway, originally designed to operate as a charabanc but also supplied with an interchangeable body. None of the North Eastern Railway's Hallfords were requisitioned during the war so its use is unknown – the caption accompanying the photograph states "arrival at Quartermaster's Stores of the Rations Van from Base", so it may have been on temporary loan from the North Eastern Railway, but not officially on the books of the War Department. The other motor vehicle shown is a Ford Model T Van, apparently in the livery of 'City Garage', which is described as the 'Billet Supply Van'.

Locomotives doing their bit

The first of the North Eastern Railway locomotives to be used for wartime activities appear to have been two L Class 0-6-0T engines, designed as a general purpose tank engine. In 1915, Number 544 was sent to Brotton in north Yorkshire, and 545 to Hartley in Northumberland, where they were used for hauling railway guns which were used for coastal defence in case of naval attack or invasion. For this role they were fitted with two Westinghouse pumps, one to serve the brakes and another to pump water from where it may be found, i.e. a trackside stream, particularly useful in an area where traditional watering facilities were not available. They were also fitted with condensing gear and train heating connections, and were painted in overall grey, which included painting over any brasswork.

Twenty North Eastern Railway locomotives went on loan to the Highland Railway for various lengths of time during the war, fifteen of them being the elderly 398 Class 0-6-0 tender locomotives, a class built between 1872 and 1884. The remaining five were BTP (Bogie Tank Passenger) locomotives, 0-4-4T designs used for branch line passenger services, the class being built between 1874 and 1884. More 398 Class locomotives were used elsewhere, six going to the Caledonian Railway and two to the London & North Western Railway. It is possible that these locomotives were lent out to cover for these railways' more modern locomotives serving abroad with the Railway Operating

Division, as would T1 Class locomotives of the North Eastern Railway. The loan of locomotives to other British railway companies continued through to peacetime – in November 1919, 18 of the 398 Class 0-6-0 locomotives were sent to the Highland Railway, and in the same period nine C Class 0-6-0 locomotives were loaned to the Taff Vale Railway in Wales, and three C Class locomotives went on loan to the Maryport & Carlisle Railway.

Other North Eastern Railway locomotives were used at munitions works – H Class 0-4-0T number 1798 worked at the Barnbow, Leeds munitions factory, and as described in the '1915' chapter, three other H Class locomotives, 129, 587 and 898 were hired for work at the Woolwich Arsenal, as well as smaller K Class 0-4-0T 559. Another H Class, 1799, saw Admiralty work at the Kyle of Lochalsh. Three each of the E and E1 class 0-6-0T shunting locomotives were fitted with spark arresters fitted to the chimneys, designed by the Hunslet Engine Company of Leeds, and put to work in various National Filling Factories – these were E Class 1789, 1834 and 1864 and E1 Class 1715, 1721 and 2179. Filling factories, as the name suggests, filled the shells produced elsewhere such as the Darlington National Projectile Factory ran by the North Eastern Railway, and were highly dangerous places – the deadliest explosion in a British munitions factory in the First World War occurred when National Filling Factory No. 6 at Chilwell, Nottinghamshire, blew up on 1 July 1918, killing 134 and injuring 250.

H1 Class 0-6-0T locomotives 590 and 995, tank engines fitted with a crane on their rear bunker, were in use at Immingham Dock in 1918 where their novel feature would have been of good use. Although still owned and operated by the North Eastern Railway, the decision was taken in 1916 to base E Class locomotive 972 at Ripon for work on the busy Ripon Camp branch, not far from where War Department locomotive 104, previously North Eastern Railway 1350 Class 0-6-0T number 1361 was based at Richmond for use in building Catterick Camp which saw massive building and expansion during the war.

By 1916, over on the Western Front, the Railway Operating Division, a unit in the Royal Engineers who, as the title suggests, operated railways, were to become responsible for more and more railway lines. The French were unable to manage following the Somme and Verdun battles of 1916 as well as domestic traffic such as the need for transporting farm produce at harvest time. At the same time the North Eastern Railway's Sir Eric Geddes, by now serving as Inspector-General of Transportation and Director-General of Military Railways as Honorary Major General had been studying whether it would be more practical for the British to be responsible for the railways serving their sectors. To do so locomotives and rolling stock were required from British railways to cope with demand, as well as locomotives being built in the USA by Baldwin and Canada by the Canadian Locomotive Company. The first of 370 locomotives requested by the Railway Executive Committee from the British railway companies were shipped in November 1916, and from then on a steady stream of goods locomotives were shipped over to France. At first, 22 P Class 0-6-0 locomotives from the North Eastern Railway were earmarked for Railway Operating Division service, and these were collected together at Borough Gardens Shed at Gateshead from October 1916 onwards and prepared for their foreign service. The P Class locomotives were designed by Wilson Worsdell and seventy were built from 1894 until 1898, designed and mainly used for short distance mineral trains, such as picking up coal trains from collieries to the nearest docks. They were very suitable for war service and similar 0-6-0 designs from other companies were also being shipped over to France, however in early 1917 the decision was made that they were not needed (possibly due to the North Eastern Railway sending their entire T1 Class), and so were returned to service.

All 50 of the T1 Class of 0-8-0 mineral locomotives were sent to France in early 1917 as part of the North Eastern Railway's contribution to the Railway Operating Division. The Ministry of Munitions had selected a heavy goods locomotive to be produced for ROD service of, the Great Central Railway's 8K Class 2-8-0, which were to be built in large numbers with the first order placed in February 1917 (over five hundred were built for the ROD) but the first of these would not be completed and shipped to France until September 1917 so there was still an immediate need for engines. The T1 Class was a development of the T Class, developed by Wilson Worsdell who was Chief Mechanical Engineer from 1890–1910 (although from 1890–1902 the role was known as 'Locomotive Superintendent') who realised towards the end of the nineteenth century that a larger type of locomotive was needed to haul the ever-increasing number and size of goods and mineral trains on the railway. The new design had to be strong and reliable, but also had to have a light axle loading for use on poor quality colliery lines and also to minimise the chance of ground subsidence over tracks which ran over mine workings. The biggest mineral engine in use at the time on the North Eastern Railway was the P1 Class 0-6-0, and looking at other railway companies, the London & North Western Railway had been successfully using 0-8-0 locomotives since 1893. It was decided to build 0-8-0 locomotives with outside cylinders and piston valves, and the first batch of ten was built at Gateshead Works in 1901, shortly followed in 1902 by another batch of ten built at Gateshead between March and June, identical to the first but with slide valves, and these were known as the T1 Class. Another thirty were built of the T Class with piston valves between 1902 and 1904. Tests were conducted in the summer of 1906 with the company's new Dynamometer Car (which went on to record the 'Mallard's speed record-breaking run for steam locomotives in 1938) to see which was better – the piston valve T class or the slide valve T1 Class. It was found that the T1 Class was superior, and so a further 40 T1 Class locomotives were built, twenty between 1908–1908 and twenty in 1911, all at the Darlington North Road Works.

The T and T1 Class 0-8-0s were joined in 1913 by the T2 Class, designed by Chief Mechanical Engineer Vincent Raven to cope with the still-increasing sizes of mineral trains. The T2 Class took the superb qualities of Worsdell's T and T1 Class even further, and with a larger boiler and superheaters fitted as standard they were very reliable and powerful enough for the heavy demands placed on them. Thirty were built at Darlington before the outbreak of war, bringing the total of 0-8-0 mineral locomotives in the North Eastern Railway's stock to 120. The loss of the entire T1 Class of fifty engines for the war effort was no small undertaking – although the company was allocated materials to build locomotives to replace these, the loss was still felt and would certainly not make it any easier on the operation and maintenance of the mineral engines already hard at work. One small consolation was that the 22 P Class locomotives which had been prepared for overseas service then stored at Borough Gardens Shed at Gateshead since October 1916 were ultimately not sent for ROD service. They were returned to service with the North Eastern Railway by March 1917 – there does not seem to be an officially recorded reason as to why they were not used, as they were similar to other 0-6-0 types used in large numbers by the ROD from other companies. It is possible that either the NER could not afford to lose them as well as the 50 T1 Class locomotives, or that the ROD felt they either had enough locomotives or could do without so as to not overly strip the NER of locomotives. The only other locomotives prepared and not sent for ROD service was a batch of twelve 0-8-0s from the Lancashire & Yorkshire Railway.

The fifty T1s were sent to France in early 1917, the locomotives being sent via Portsmouth as there were cranes available at the Royal Navy dockyard large enough to lift them, and they arrived at Le Havre where, again, there were suitable cranes to offload them. Percy Rosewarne, quoted above, was one of those who took the T1s down to Portsmouth – what follows is his account of the trip:

On duty 12 noon 'waiting orders'. My mate was Jack Leeming and I had not been booked for the turn but while I was in bed I was sent a 'ticket' saying 'Book on 12.0 noon: spare'. On duty I learned that seven engines were on the road to Portsmouth, en-route for France.

The first two came at 4.0 pm and we went first engine. Food at that time was very hard to get and I had only two shillings in my pocket. As far as we knew we had to work them to Mexborough. Both engines were new from overhaul at the Works and they were a picture to behold. My mate and I checked over the list of engine equipment – ninety-eight articles in all – and everything brand new. I had never seen so much equipment before or since. All new mahogany seats in the cab and all side cab window frames. Three new headlamps, two handlamps and a gauge lamp.

Our orders were to run at a speed of 25 mph. At Mexborough there was no relief but another pilotman, and so the day became far spent until we came to Woodford. A guide took us to our lodgings and we booked off for eight hours. There was no food available and we went up to bed only to find that two men were in. As they got out we moved in and I slept until we were knocked up. A wash and then out on to the streets to look for food. I was lucky and got one pork pie, the only food I had had for about fourteen hours.

We prepared the engine and off we went again; pilotman after pilotman came on, all were amazed at the engine, the cab and its fittings. The comfortable seats, steam reverse, and brake all to the driver's hand. Dewrance's boiler gauge fittings and Gresham's Combination Injectors. The tender coalway, with its good shovelling plate and removable boards giving access to all the coal, was something to be proud of. Still no food available and so for the rest of that day we went hungry.

We arrived in Portsmouth in fine style because at some point during the night we had to wait and all seven engines were coupled together. Seven 'Geordies' all in a line. What a photograph it would have made!

We had a few hours sleep and were given a little food, and with one permit to cover all the men we boarded a train for London. There we walked all the way to King's Cross, buying any food we saw. Jack Cook, No. 1, a well-known Yorkshire bred lad, with big basket and leather strap over his shoulder, led the way. The sun was shining and we caused some comment. At one point we came to a halt, not sure of the way to go. Jack looked around at the fine buildings and said, in broad Yorkshire 'Tha nivver naws where yan gets to when yan gets away from yam'. London stopped and all eyes were turned on us.... We arrived back in York shed at 11.30pm on Saturday after the longest shift I ever worked

The exact arrival dates of the T1s into France are not known, however by summer at least four are known to have been in service and are recorded at Bergues in July and August (ten miles south east of Dunkirk on the Nord line to Hazebrouck then onwards to the junction of the military line to Proven and then onwards to the Ypres Salient, the focus of July-November 1917). On arrival it was found that the quickly laid and generally poor quality military railway lines were not suitable for the T1s to run on as they were too heavy, and so they were replaced as soon as possible by lighter locomotives. However they did still appear on these lines as necessity brought their use about. Instead, the T1s would be found further behind the lines used for the heavy haulage of goods and mineral traffic – exactly the work they had been designed for at the start of the century. The locomotives were painted in grey, with white lettering and numbering. At first they kept their original numbers, but with the large numbers of locomotives coming into ROD service from British railway companies there was bound to be conflicting numbers soon. The first locomotives to be renumbered were those numbered 643–661, whose numbers were increased by 5000 to avoid confliction with North British Railway locomotives. Later, to standardise the numbering, the ROD locomotives were numbered in series, and the new build Baldwin 0-6-0T locomotives from the USA became numbered 651–700, which meant that all T1 locomotives numbered in that series also had their numbers increased by 5000, if they had not been already by the confliction with NBR locomotives.

The T1s quickly won the respect of the ROD crews and became known as the most popular of the ROD locomotives to work on owing to the same features which caused praise to be lavished on them by the pilotmen described by Percy Rosewarne on the transportation of the T1s to Portsmouth. The neat steam reverser was one feature often particularly mentioned, but perhaps the main positive feature of the T1s was the particularly comfortable cab, especially compared to other cabs with more limited vision and much more open. The large front and side windows gave superb visibility, and the large cab as a whole was a pleasant aspect for the crew, where space was at a premium. It is not believed that the T1s were involved in any serious accidents or suffered as a result of enemy action during their ROD service, although it is recorded that 1002 was derailed at Mendinghem on 7 August 1917, and 774 was repaired at St Etienne-Du-Rouvray in July 1918. Apart from these incidents however their service record is mostly unblemished and they did their work just as they did before the war, reliably and dependably.

The return of the T1s after the war was remarked upon by J. W. Sinton of the Goods Department at South Shields, writing;

> I saw them pass as I stood gazing out of the window, and wondered how long it would be before I followed them.
>
> They were worth looking at, those war-scarred engines. Anyone who was worked amongst locomotives will know how I felt. There is a sort of human emotion in their bowels, and I have heard enginemen speak of particular locomotives in terms of endearment such as one finds in the stable and kennels.
>
> There was a whole train-load, and, travelling as they were without steam, they looked tired to the point of weariness. It seemed, as I

watched them pass, they moved proudly, yet not unwilling to accept aid from one of their own species which had borne the strain of extra work at home.

Running my eye quickly along the train for one I knew, I easily picked out the famous Worsdell cab, which gives the symmetrical touch to what is perhaps the finest model in the world. On the side of each tender were the letters "R.O.D." and a number.

When the T1s returned to the North Eastern Railway between February and July 1919, the railway was justifiably proud of the locomotive's service just as they had been of their men who served. To commemorate the T1s service, the locomotives were fitted with a brass replica of the insignia of the Royal Engineers, the flaming grenade with nine flames. Below the Royal Engineers insignia, there were three brass chevrons – these chevrons mimicked the overseas service stripes introduced in 1918 as part of the uniform of British soldiers – each stripe represented one year's overseas service, and so the T1's (although possibly not all of them, as the dates they were sent to France are not confirmed) had earned three stripes for their service from 1917 to 1919. The Royal Engineers' badge and three years overseas service stripes were affixed to the cab sides, below the windows and above the Works plate detailing the locomotive's place of manufacture, year of manufacture and locomotive number. When the London & North Eastern Railway repainted the T1 Class locomotives in the 1920s and the locomotive number was painted on the cab side, the insignia was moved to the front wheel splasher.

Despite the return of the fifty T1 class locomotives in 1919, the opportunity was taken in 1919 to hire thirty-three of the ROD Class 2-8-0 locomotives from the Ministry of Transport. 521 in total were built from 1917 onwards, and after the war were put into storage – some of them not seeing war service at all, being built too late to be sent to France or elsewhere where they could be of use. A number were sold, including some which went as far afield as Australia, but there was still a large surplus so they were put up for loan to British railway companies. Eight of these came unused from storage, and another seven came straight from the manufacturers, who were still building them as late as May 1920 despite the war being over, as the contracts were still running for their manufacture. The remaining locomotives came from storage in Surrey, and were locomotives that had served in France. They were all returned in August 1921. Some North Eastern Railway men were already familiar with the ROD 2-8-0 locomotives – after the war, photographs of ROD locomotives were published in the *North Eastern Railway Magazine*, and amongst them was a photograph of ROD 2-8-0 number 1988, which was driven by Corporal J. G. Dunn and Corporal W. Skelton of the ROD – both were firemen on the North Eastern Railway pre-war at Tyne Dock. Other North Eastern Railway men in the ROD included Sergeant G. E. Mawson and Sapper R. Errington – Driver and Fireman respectively on the same locomotive in France, a Beyer Peacock of Manchester locomotive employed on hauling ambulance trains in France and Belgium. Both worked together in pre-war days on the railway, and mentioned that as far as they were aware, they were the only case of a pre-war footplate crew being abroad together. The Beyer Peacock locomotive they served on was one of fourteen 4-6-4T express passenger tank engines, originally built as part of an order for thirty-four for the Dutch State Railway pre-war, but not delivered owing to the decline of railway traffic in neutral Holland. They were amongst the first ROD locomotives to arrive from Britain, and when they were replaced on supply trains by more suitable heavy freight locomotives from British railway companies, were transferred to work on civilian, troop and ambulance trains. Their steam heating made them popular in this role, and their large cabs made them popular with their crews, especially as it could double as sleeping accommodation if needed.

Rolling stock, rails and Tugs

Although it was not until 1917 that any of the North Eastern Railway's locomotives were called up for foreign service, as early as 1914 two of the Company's steam-powered breakdown cranes joined the war effort. One was CME 1, a 15-ton capacity crane built by Cowans Sheldon of Carlisle in 1893 at a cost of £5,550 – the breakdown cranes that went to the War were used not just for recovering locomotives and rolling stock in the event of accident such as a derailment (although they would have been particularly useful for this on the relatively poorly laid down railway lines on the Western Front), but also for heavy lifting and construction work. The other North Eastern Railway steam breakdown crane was CME16, a more modern design built by Craven Brothers at Manchester in 1912 at a cost of £3,020 with a 35 ton capacity, and requisitioned from its base at Gateshead. Another 35-ton crane was built by Cowans & Sheldon in 1916 for the North Eastern Railway, likely as a replacement for CME16. CME16 stayed in Europe after the end of the war, and ended up working for the National Belgian Railway Company (known as the SNCB – Société Nationale des Chemins de fer Belges) which was formed in 1926. It was finally retired in 1985 and is now preserved in the SNCB's museum. As of November 2012 CME16 is in the museum's reserve collection store at Leuven.

4,547 railway wagons were also sent overseas as part of the contribution to the war-effort in France, and twenty-seven miles of railway line were taken up from the North Eastern Railway to be re-laid on the Western Front. On top of the contribution of railway material, rolling stock and road vehicles, six of the North Eastern Railway's steam tugs, used at the various ports on the North Eastern Railway system, were hired to the Admiralty. As detailed in the '1915' chapter, the tug *Stranton*, renamed HMS *Char,* sank with all hands on 24 January 1915. Of the others, it is known that *Seaton*, built by J. P. Rennoldson in 1899 and formerly based at West Hartlepool, was in Admiralty service from 17 November 1914 until 13 March 1919 and known as HMS *Ceylon. William Gray*, built by J. P. Rennoldson in 1911 and registered at Middlesbrough was hired from October 1914 to 1920, and North Eastern Railway No. 3, again built by J. P. Rennoldson and launched in October 1915, was hired by the Admiralty from 20 October 1915 until 22 August 1919. NER No. 3 served as HMS *Nero* at the Greek port of Mudros on the island of Lemnos, which was the base of the Naval Operations during the ill-fated Gallipoli campaign. Following the failure and evacuation of the Gallipoli peninsula, Mudros was the base for the naval blockade of the Dardanelles until the Ottoman Empire signed an armistice on the island in October 1918.

Dogs of war

It was not just men and metal of the North Eastern Railway that did their bit at the front – some horses were also attached to the 17th Battalion Northumberland Fusiliers, formed from NER men, and NER Police dogs did too. The North Eastern Railway Police had been using dogs, pioneering their use in the UK, as early as 1908 following Geddes seeing dogs working at Ghent Docks in 1906. After discussion and investigation as to the application of dogs in a policing role, the North Eastern Railway Police Southern Division started to use Airedales in 1908 at Hull Docks and Riverside Quay, the first four being named Jim, Vic, Mick and Ben. They were a success and were followed by the Northern Division using them by 1912 at Hartlepool, Tyne Dock and Middlesbrough. The kennels for the dogs were located at Hull and this is also where they were trained. They would be used only at night and trained to protect anyone in Police uniform, but soon learnt not to growl at North Eastern Railway Policemen not in uniform, despite being trained to attack anyone not in Police clothing. They even had their own uniform, a coat for bad weather. At the start of the war the Red Cross planned to use dogs as ambulance, equipped with medical supplies, but the idea was dropped early on in 1914, and in the same year Lieutenant Colonel E. H. Richardson was training dogs, especially Airedales who proved well suited for the role, as sentry and patrol dogs. In late 1916 two Airedales were trialled as message carriers for the Royal Field Artillery and by early 1917 kennels were being set up under the control of the Royal Engineers (who were responsible for Signals during the Great War, the Royal Corps of Signals was not formed until 1920) for handling message dogs. The dogs originally came from dog homes, but then as demand grew stray dogs were sent over, and then police dogs and dogs from the general public were sent over, especially owing to the difficulties in keeping them with rationing in effect by 1918. The Airedales of the North Eastern Railway Police were amongst those sent over, especially as Airedales were one of the more favoured breeds for this role, as well as Border Collies and Lurchers.

The dogs carried messages in metal tins on a special collar around the dog's neck, and would be kept near the front line and used to run to and from headquarters behind the lines – it was an offence to stop a dog in its duty, and were used alongside the more better known carrier pigeons. On the other side of no man's land, the Germans were using Alsatians, and interestingly after the war in 1923 it was decided to use Alsatians instead of Airedales.

Women in North Eastern Railway Service

In view of the large number of platform porters who have joined His Majesty's forces, and to liberate other men wishful to enlist, the Company decided, as a temporary experimental arrangement, to employ women porters at stations such as York, Darlington, Middlesbrough, Leeds, Hull, West Hartlepool, Stockton and Newcastle.

North Eastern Railway Magazine, 1915

As the above quote records, owing to staff shortages as Reservists, Territorials and then other staff members left to join armed forces, by 1915 it was found necessary that women would undertake more front-line roles on the North Eastern Railway to replace the men that had left for the duration of the war. In total, the number of women and girls employed on the North Eastern Railway increased from 1,470 before the war to a total of 7,885, without including over 1,000 more employed at the NER-run Darlington National Projectile Factory. By January 1915 there were already four female clerks working in the parcels office at Newcastle (this number rising to sixteen by late 1916). It was mentioned at the time of this announcement that although the employment of women and girls on railways may be a novelty to some companies, it certainly was not to the North Eastern Railway – in 1849 there were female stationmasters at Thornley and Castle Eden Colliery (by 1915 known as Hesleden) stations, both in County Durham. In other locations:

The collector at Ouseburn Bridge between Byker and Heaton (then used by foot passengers) was also a woman, who fulfilled the duties of the post for 18s. per week. Women acted as gatekeepers at High Stoop and Blackfield on the Wear Valley Railway, the wages of the one being 10d. per day and those of the other 6d. per day. Early in the 'seventies a staff of young women was engaged in connection with the Audit Department to sort out the tickets which had been collected from passengers.

In 1877 a platelayer's daughter performed the duties of a stationmaster at Elrington for 2s. per week. She and her brother, a platelayer, who assisted her at times in her work, occupied the station house rent free. And, finally, in the 'eighties we find a railwayman's daughter in charge of the occasional station of Smeaton..

Despite these interesting claims to the early engagement of women in railway work, the sheer numbers of women that would work for the North Eastern Railway and all other British railways during the war years brought about a much bigger change than these historically noteworthy women. By 7 February 1915 West Hartlepool station had twenty-eight female members of staff, distributed as follows:

2 working in the stationmaster's office
2 in the telegraph office
4 in the booking office
5 in the parcels office
6 platform porters
2 ticket collectors
1 left luggage porter
6 carriage cleaners

Following this information in the *North Eastern Railway Magazine* was another interesting statement extolling the virtues of female staff:

As in all other capacities women have come forward splendidly to take up railway duties in various grades so that the male staff may be liberated for the defence of their King and Country, and, considering the fact that they are entirely strange to railway work, every credit is due to them for the manner in which they are tackling the various duties required with a view to becoming speedily efficient.

There was also the matter of clothing for the new staff as they entered a previously male only occupation. The smart uniform consisted of a long dark skirt with dark long jacket, with a light coloured shirt. This was topped off with a peaked cap, although photos show some members of staff wearing wide brimmed caps, possibly denoting a more senior member of staff. By 1915 there were also bus conductresses on the North Eastern Railway's motor bus services – all around the country conductresses were appearing on bus and tram services, and the NER was no exception. Lily White was one of the NER Conductresses and worked on the route between Harton and South Shields.

By early 1915 there were even dedicated Ladies Ambulance Classes, the first being held at Bishop Auckland, and even the North Eastern Railway Rifle Clubs had Ladies Clubs – in March 1915 the Darlington North Eastern Railway Rifle Club had a shooting match with the Gateshead NER Ladies Rifle Club. The clerks employed at York at this time had formed a hockey club in order to keep fit and to counteract "the enervating effects of a sedentary life". The club was called the 'Brooklands Club', playing matches on Saturday afternoons and captained by Miss Hilda Banks, vice-captain being Miss L Etherington and secretary & treasurer Miss E. W. Grimshaw. Continuing the sporting theme, the female munitions workers at the NER ran Darlington National Projectile Factory had their own football team, as detailed in the relevant chapter.

An article and accompanying photograph published in early 1916 in the *North Eastern Railway Magazine* detailed the work of female labourers working at Middlesbrough docks. They worked casually when demand required it, up to thirty-nine women in one day being employed in the charging, weighing, stencilling, sorting and storing cargo. They were especially involved in the unloading of 20,000 bags of prize coffee from the cargo ships SS *Drottning Sophia* and SS *Forde*.

On 25 May 1916 the first women engine-cleaners started work at the York shed, about a year after the first women platform porters started work. The need for women engine-cleaners, which was unsurprisingly a particularly dirty job, came about as:

Like many other industries the war created a shortage in suitable youths for the cleaning sheds at York, and, consequently, serious consideration had to be given to the employment of female labour. This was at last decided upon and after suitable accommodation had been provided, York shed was 'invaded' for the first time by female labour on May 25 1916. The ladies quickly adapted themselves to the work and the fact that their numbers have been augmented proves the venture was a success as at other stations. In the beginning their labours were confined to No. 4 shed, but before long their sphere of industry was extended to the whole of the sheds. Altogether 40 are now employed.

As will be seen in the photograph the ladies look very workmanlike in their costumes and cause no small stir as they take their after-dinner walk along Leeman Road.

The above was written by an anonymous writer, published in the *North Eastern Railway Magazine*, 1916. The article notes that women engine cleaners are already at work at other sheds, with photos published of them in previous editions showing them working at Neville Hill, Leeds and Middlesbrough. The editor also states that:

The photographs will not only serve as a record of women's part in the great war, but will also have an interest for North Eastern soldiers in the trenches and elsewhere, among whom, we believe, the Magazine has a considerable circulation, and who will be pleased to see how the women are "carrying on" the important work of the railway during their absence.

It is fortunate indeed that the magazine published so many photographs of women employed on vital war work on the North Eastern Railway, not just of cleaners but also porters and munitions workers at the Darlington Munitions Factory amongst other roles, and act as superb reminders of the important work done. The rapid social change that women experienced during the First World War in regard to work and rights is shown in a phrase which seems bizarre to modern eyes:

For such work as that of lady's maid to a locomotive, trousers are obviously the "only wear." ... it is not easy to grasp that the engine is a real one and that the women are doing real hard work in the place of their menfolk in the fighting line.

Women wearing trousers was a big 'shock' which came about during the First World War – prior to this even bicycles and motorcycles for women were designed differently, with drop-frames to allow women wearing skirts to ride them. Utilitarian clothing was needed to be worn by women for the manual work they were now doing, not just cleaning railway engines but working in munitions factories.

The employing of women as clerks also caused some debate in 1916 in the Great Western Railway's magazine as to the correct term – either 'Female Clerk', Woman Clerk' or 'Girl Clerk' – however all of these suggestions came from males, and the editor of the *North Eastern Railway Magazine* hinted that "it would be interesting to hear from the feminine staff themselves how they would prefer to be referred to".

Aside from correspondence published as to the correct terminology for the new members of staff, the Great Western Railway magazine did make a case for the advantages of female staff;

> The average female clerk's strongest point is her temperament. In this she excels the male for patient application to details in monotonous duties and rule-of-thumb work. From childhood she cultivates this disposition. What boy or man would have enough patience to sit hour after hour making tiny stitches in sewing, knitting or crotcheting? Yet this is a pleasing pastime to girls. Typewriting is not far removed from this kind of work, and the female clerk can contentedly ply her art at the typewriter until her last letter is written, without feeling obliged to break off occasionally to stand with her back to the fire and talk about sports, politics, or the conduct of the war.

In response to this article published in the *North Eastern Railway Magazine*, two replies from female staff members at Newcastle Central were soon received. The first was from someone referred to as just 'L.A.' and objected to 'Woman Clerk' on the terms that it sounded like "a portly old dame, anxious to do her bit as a war-worker" and 'Girl Clerk" as it suggested "an unsophisticated female of the 'flapper' type". 'L.A.' preferred the term 'Female Clerk', and also remarked that:

It seems rather unfair that our male colleagues should judge us on quite the same footing as themselves, as in many cases they are inclined to lose sight of the fact that our advent into the railway world has been somewhat hurried and consequently we have not had the advantage of a long probationary period to fit us for filling adequately the positions vacated by the men who have answered 'the call'.

Then, again, we must remember that in pre-war times, we women figured rather in the light of subordinates leaving the positions of responsibility to the men, with the result that in these times of urgent need we have, at a moment's notice, to cease being a figure of secondary importance and assume positions which hitherto we deemed quite beyond our capabilities."

The other correspondent, 'J.B.', also preferred the term 'Female Clerk' and wrote:

Who, a year or two ago, would have believed that women would ever have been permitted to assist in shipyards, or to sweep the streets, or act as post-women, porters or ticket collectors, to say nothing of the clerical grade? Certainly not the male population, and it is mainly due to the advent of the war that so many openings have occurred for the willing female worker. I think the men will at least allow that if not as physically capable as themselves women, at any rate, are very courageous in trying to do their bit by endeavouring to carry the business of the country on, and cultivate the land so that all the men available may be released for active service.

'J.B.' also agreed with the viewpoint of 'L.A.' regarding the efficiency of female clerks:

It must be taken into consideration that while the men who have been in the service several years have been trained from their boyhood, most of the females have only been training a few months, and therefore it is hardly fair to draw comparisons, even though it be admitted that a girl's intuitive powers are keener than a prosaic man's.

By autumn 1916 there were twenty women employed by the North Eastern Railway at Hull Paragon station, not including clerks, and their various roles included porters, telegraph messengers, letter sorting and number taking – with the contributor from Hull Paragon station J. E. Elliott commenting that "the work they have been called upon to do has been performed better than expected". A photo published in the December 1916 edition of the *North Eastern Railway Magazine* showed a number of women at the Leeds Neville Hill engine shed on an R1 Class locomotive – there was a great deal of interest in this photograph, and amongst the number of letters received regarding the photograph was one from the Secretary of the 'Bureau of Railway News and Statistics' of Chicago asking for permission to reproduce the photograph in their annual report. Another photograph in the January 1917 edition of lady clerks in the passenger and goods department at Spennymore station was referred to in the next month's edition, the editor writing:

> Judging from comments which reach us, group photographs of the feminine staff are a popular feature of the magazine. Those published last month elicited many expressions of appreciation.

The photographs continued to come in, and those of engine cleaners especially show a great variety in the locations and types of locomotives – two of the more interesting locomotives both come from Shildon, one showing women cleaners on a T or T1 Class locomotive and another showing them on one of the brand new powerful electric freight locomotives, recently introduced onto the newly electrified Shildon to Newport line in 1915.

The North Eastern Railway Police suffered heavily from loss of staff during the war, exactly half joining the armed forces (a 1916 figure gives 339 members of the force, presumably including those away in the armed forces), so it was decided that women would be allowed to join the force. It was the North Eastern Railway that instigated the use of railway policewomen, however by the time the first were sworn in, the Great Western Railway and Great Eastern Railway already had some working for them. The first four were appointed in November 1917, and a further thirteen were sworn in at the York City Police Court on 23 May 1918. The women served under Sergeant M. Roberts and had a smart uniform, again with a long skirt and jacket like the porters, with a wide brimmed hat, whistle and shirt with collar and tie, and duty bands on the left wrist of the jacket.

As well as the munitions workers at the North Eastern Railway run Darlington National Projectile Factory, the North Eastern Railway also employed female munitions workers at the York Telegraph Workshops, where primers for firing artillery shells were repaired for re-use. The work was described in early 1918, by which time this work had been undertaken for around two years:

> The work is of a delicate nature, for there are no less than sixteen different operations on the primer before they are completed and ready for the refilling factories, and the finished primers must not in any one respect vary from the micrometer standard to a greater extent than 1/1000th of an inch. The machines used have been perfect to the point of simplicity, and are operated by the girls with great dexterity.

The large numbers of women now working on the railways, not just on the North Eastern Railway, but on other railways around the country, had increased to a point where a Railway Women's Convalescent Home was opened at Lavenham in Suffolk in the summer of 1918 – convalescent homes for railwaymen were already existing and provided a place for them to go when recovering from sickness or other ill health.

Towards the end of the war one photograph of a female porter earned her a prize – a photograph of Mrs Heppell, a temporary porter at Haxby, sent a photograph of herself in North Eastern Railway uniform complete with peaked cap to the *Weekly Telegraph* for entry in a beauty competition, and won the prize of £5. Mrs Heppell had been in the employ of the North Eastern Railway since 7 February 1916, and her competition success was reported in the May 1919 edition of the *North Eastern Railway Magazine*, remarking that "the uniform she wears, though sufficiently becoming, was not chosen for effect, but is the ordinary clothing of her calling"

With the war over, men that survived and were fit to return to work did so after being demobilised, and the temporary women workers left their posts. There were plenty of leaving parties and presentations of gifts to those leaving, who by and large had enjoyed their work and were sad to leave, although fully aware that this would be the situation and the terms of their employment.

With the numbers of women workers decreasing, the Women's Welfare Department closed at the end of 1919. The assistant welfare supervisor for the southern area, Miss G. E. Hollam, had already left in early 1919 after starting her role in July 1917. Miss Hollam left to take up a post as the head of a ladies club in the west end of London, remarking that she had enjoyed her job but as the work was decreasing she thought it best to accept a permanent post when the opportunity came up and she was offered it. Originally set up to look after the welfare of the many women now working on the North Eastern Railway, the Department was run by Miss Arnold-Forster who took up her duties as welfare supervisor in April 1917, including the munitions workers in the Darlington National Projectile Factory. Upon her leaving, Miss Arnold Forster wrote a letter to be published in the *North Eastern Railway Magazine*:

> I shall not forget the women and girls amongst whom I have worked, who came forward so splendidly to the help of the nation, by undertaking work on the line that no one had ever imagined women could do. Nor shall I forget the way in which they stuck to it, and my admiration and respect has been great for many – especially the married women, who managed to keep good time, did their work well and then went home to do a week's washing or spent their spare hours cleaning or mending.

Miss A. S. Dickson, the assistant supervisor for the northern area, left on the same day as Miss Arnold-Forster, on 31 December 1919, closing the Women's Welfare Department. This effectively brought to a close the years of superb service given to the North Eastern Railway by women who came in their thousands to free men from vital occupations for the armed forces. They had in to a workplace completely different from anything they had done before yet took to their roles quickly and highly competently.

The North Eastern Railway Battalion – 17th (Pioneer) Battalion, Northumberland Fusiliers

"The Boys of the N.E.R."

Along our line, from Hull to Tyne
And north to the Berwick wall
A signal ran
To every man,
"Do you hear your Country call?"

(CHORUS)

Hurrah! Hurrah! Hurrah!
For the Boys of the N.E.R.
Who are now enrolled
In the "Old and Bold"
And keen to go to War.

From every grade, to England's aid,
Went twice two thousand – then
A thousand more
To form a corps
Of all North Eastern Men

(CHORUS)

So here's to all who heard that call
To fight across the foam.
And here's to "The Day"
When blithe and gay
They'll all come marching home.

(CHORUS)

Soon after war broke out, Eric Geddes approached the War Office to offer the services of a fully trained unit of men for railway work, made up of civilian railway men. The War Office turned down the offer as they were confident it would not be needed, however did allow the North Eastern Railway to organise the raising of a Battalion of men from within the company, similar to 'Pals' units created in mainly industrial areas to encourage men to join so that they could serve with their friends. On 8 September a circular went around the railway notifying staff of the proposed formation of a North Eastern Railway Battalion'.

By this time, one in ten North Eastern Railway men were already 'with the colours', which was higher than the national estimated average of one in thirty railwaymen by this date. Despite this, the response was higher than anyone expected, and replies to the circular, by way of a completed form at the bottom of the circular, flooded in. 1,100 men were required, and within several days almost triple that amount had applied to serve in the Battalion.

Raising, formation and training

Just three days after the circular went out, on 11 September formal sanction from Lord Kitchener himself was given for the formation of the 17th (North Eastern Railway) Battalion Northumberland Fusiliers. On 14 September recruitment started at the York Railway Institute, with recruiting also open at the Newcastle Railway Institute the next day, alternating between York and Newcastle each day. By 23 September the formation of the North Eastern Railway Battalion was 'practically a thing accomplished'. The medical examination of the men happened on the day of recruiting, which consisted of a basic test, which involved ensuring they were no shorter than 5 feet and 6 inches and had a chest measurement of not less than 35 ½ inches. Following successful completion of this they were passed on to Major H. A. Watson, the NER General Superintendent, who attested them into the Battalion.

The Battalion was to be housed and trained at King George Dock at Hull, which was jointly owned by the NER and the Hull & Barnsley Railway, opened on 26th June 1914 by King George V and with some buildings still barely used, and with the drop in coastal shipping trade this meant the men and their equipment could easily be accommodated. Number 5 and Number 6 Warehouses (joined together on the ground floor) were to be used, the first detachment of the Battalion arriving on 22 September, with the entire Battalion on site by 1 October. The upper floor of the warehouses contained the lavatories and sleeping quarters for the men, whilst the ground floor was home to two dining halls for the men. The ground floor also had an indoor miniature rifle range, armoury and armourer's office, recreation hall, drill hall, kitchen, guard room and other rooms. The Officers' quarters were on the Hull & Netherlands Steamship Company's vessel SS *Rievaulx Abbey* which was moored alongside the warehouses. The recreation hall was filled with every sort of indoor game imaginable, and for the entire war the Battalion was receiving gifts from the NER railway staff, often including games. A letter to the *North Eastern Railway Magazine* in 1914 from Colonel D. B. Preston who was commanding the Battalion read:

> Will you allow me through the North Eastern Railway Magazine to say how grateful all ranks of the North Eastern Railway Battalion are for the numerous gifts received from many kind donors.

Outside the warehouses, there was an area of open ground enclosed by buildings which was suitable for drill and manoeuvres, although as it was covered in rough ballast it was soon found more suitable to use a field at nearby Saltend. The daily march to this, consisting of several miles, helped to swiftly get the men into shape. The typical day-to-day life of a new recruit at Hull was as follows:

0530 – Reveille. Get up, dress, wash in cold water, roll up bedding, and then head down to the dining halls for coffee and biscuits.

0630 – First parade.

0745 – Breakfast, followed by delivery of letters by orderlies.

0900–1230 – Parade (which would include training *etc.*) followed by lunch, then another parade until 1630 when tea would be served, after which the recruits had the day to themselves until 'lights out' unless they had duties to perform such as guard duty.

With the large numbers of men joining the Army at the outbreak of war, demand for the khaki Service Dress uniforms soon outstripped supply, and the NER Battalion was no exception. The men trained in their civilian clothes with a white armband showing their new status as soldiers at first, and later on were issued with blue jerseys to give some semblance of uniformity. The uniforms and personal kit, including rifles, was fully issued by 14 November, with a full complement of equipment by 2 December. Certainly the North Eastern Railway wherever it could – horse drawn vehicles built a the York Carriage & Wagon Workshops were marked as belonging to the 17th Battalion Northumberland Fusiliers before leaving York, so this may have been some sort of deal with the War Office.

Part way through November the men were confined to barracks and were not allowed to send letters – this state of affairs meant rumours abounded as to what was happening. It appeared likely the Battalion was to move, but to where? Rumours did not just consist of Belgium and France – Egypt and far-flung parts of the British Empire were popular possible destinations. The answer came on 18 November when most of the Battalion entrained at 1400 for an unknown destination, a few hours later arriving there – rural East Yorkshire. The men sent here (a small contingent remained at Hull) were put on coastal defence duties in the area around Easingston and Kilnsea. The threat of invasion was foremost in many minds, and by the time Number 11 Platoon arrived in Easington, the men were 'in a highly excited state, thinking the Germans had landed on the east coast, and expecting them to jump out of every hedge".

Whilst the NER Battalion was based in this area, the Quartermaster's Stores were based in a Primitive Methodist Hall. Photographs of this time show deliveries from a civilian Ford Model T van, evidently coming from 'City Garage', possibly in Hull, and a North Eastern Railway 1908 Hallford motor van delivering stores to the billets. The men were to stay in the area for around three months, some fortunate to be billeted in houses. Some less fortunate were billeted in an old fisherman's hut with an old boat forming the roof. The typical routine for coastal defence duties would be one night and one day on duty at the coast, alternating between sentry duty and patrolling the coast. Following this there would be one day and one night in reserve, then one day and one night guarding the village, with half a day's rest and then back on coastal duty.

Trenches were also dug and were to be manned with rifles loaded, and barbed wire defences set up. Long, boring spells of duty mixed with fresh, eager new recruits resulted in plenty of stories about spies (one supposedly looking rather conspicuous in a swallow-tailed coat and trilby hat) and landing Germans. The slightest movement, either real of perceived by a bored mind, became a full blown enemy landing – on one occasion a lost Officer of the Battalion was shot at, but fortunately not hit, by a sentry after detecting movement and then seeing the light of a torch. Inanimate objects were shot by excitable soldiers, and a large black dog who created a scare very narrowly avoided the same fate.

The East Coast bombardment of 16 December 1914 proved that employing troops in coastal defence was not folly. As the Army and Royal Navy were aware of the impending attack, at 0130 support and reserve troops were brought up from the rear areas to man the trenches by the coast in case the enemy landed, although at the time most of the men thought it was another practice.

The new year brought about a change of role for the NER Battalion – owing to the men's former employment with the North Eastern Railway, and the senior Officers of the 32nd Division (which the NER Battalion was in) being impressed with the defences built on the coast. It was decided that the 17th Battalion Northumberland Fusiliers would be the Pioneer Battalion of the Division – although they could, and would, still act as a standard Infantry Battalion when needed, they would primarily be used for construction and engineering work. The change of role had one main advantage for the men – an increase in pay, two pence a day extra for Privates. On 8th February the Battalion returned to Hull where training continued in preparation for being sent overseas. A typical day by now started with an 0450 reveille, followed by half an hour of marching at the double, then breakfast. Musketry (rifle lessons/live firing), platoon drill, bayonet fighting and physical exercise filled the morning before dinner. Visual training and section drill tended to finish off the day before tea, with occasional night time lectures. As preparation for their role as Pioneer Battalion the men practised plate-laying on the railway line at Hessle, and around this time there was an increase in the length of route marches, as well as conducting more night time training. They left Hull on 20 June, entraining to Brough Park at Catterick Bridge where it joined the 96th Brigade of the 32nd Division. After five weeks they moved to Bardon Moor in Lower Wharfedale and were used to build rifle ranges. The construction of the rifle ranges involved use of a light railway to built a wide trench and embankment behind the fifty-six targets, needing to excavate, transport and pile up around ten to fifteen thousand tons of earth.

In late August 1915 the Battalion moved to Salisbury Plain where training became more prolonged and intense in the final preparation for shipping to the continent. In November, Sir Alexander Kaye Butterworth the General Manager of the North Eastern Railway travelled down to say goodbye to the men. Shortly afterwards on 20 November 1915 the Battalion (apart from the Transport and Machine Gun sections) entrained for Southampton, embarking on the SS *Empress Queen*

France

The SS *Empress Queen* arrived at Le Havre early on the morning of 21 November 1915, and after disembarking the men spent one day and night in a rest camp before commencing the march towards the front line. On 24 November they were joined by the Transport and Machine Gun sections, and arrived in the Somme valley on 27 November, billeting in the local area. D Company departed for attachment to the 51st Division at Bouzincourt, with A, B and C Companies going to Freshencourt. A, B and C Companies were attached to the 18th Division until they, and the rest of the 32nd Division, had worked up in terms of experience to the task of taking over a stretch of front line themselves.

The Battalion entered trenches on 2 December to undertake vital work such as draining, wiring, and building or improving dug outs. The first man of the Battalion to be killed was on 23 December 1915, Teddy Marsden of D Company who was killed by an enemy shell and buried the next day. By 2 January 1916 the 32nd Division was considered suitable for taking over a stretch of front line, and relieved the 51st Division which D Company had been attached to. The new year saw A Company and half of C Company making roads, B Company making dug outs and improving trenches, the other half of C Company draining land and building iron shelters, and the rest of D Company improving trenches and doing some work on trench tramways. At this stage, the narrow gauge trench tramways were not using locomotives, but were very lightly built with small, often flat wagons either pushed by men or hauled by a single mule/horse.

The road A Company was working on was for preparation of the 'Big Push', which would become known as the Battle of the Somme. After its first two months in France, the NER Battalion had losses of six men killed and nine wounded.

Towards the end of January 1916 there were rumours of a German attack, so the Machine Gun Section, equipped with the Lewis light machine gun, took over emplacements behind the front line on 29 January to back up the troops already there. Despite a violent artillery duel between both sides on 31 January, there was no German attack and so they returned to the Battalion. The use of the Machine Gun Section to back up existing troops showed the versatility of the Pioneer Battalions – as well as doing important work, they were also a very useful reserve to plug a gap in the line or bolster defences, especially the machine gunners.

By 11 February the Battalion was at Albert in billets, mainly working on roads and shelters at Crucifix Corner, Aveluy. The shelters were extremely strong dug-outs built into a steep bank, designed to withstand heavy shells. During this period some men were able to get leave, although the time taken to return to the north east meant a return home wasn't always a viable option. St George's Day was celebrated with a sports day as was traditional for the Northumberland Fusiliers – sports included wrestling whilst bareback on a mule. Twenty-four men of the Transport Section took part in this particular event, and it was won by Private J. Mounsey. Another sport was the moving of a barbed wire entanglement six feet long and three feet high. This could be done using materials found in the trenches such as sandbags, ladders, sheets of corrugated iron and poles.

A Company broke a record for railway laying in April, whilst working on the railway at Vecquemont. During one day from 0700 until 2200 they were able to lay a length of standard gauge railway one mile and thirty yards long, the previous employment of the men no doubt being a major contributing factor in the speed at which this was done.

The Big Push

During the 'Big Push', due to occur in the Summer of 1916, the NER Battalion was to be held in reserve. The plan was for It to be used to open up communication lines between the British front line and captured ground. During the bombardment in the days leading up to the attack, the Battalion repaired and took control of trench tramways, and also took over five saps made by tunnellers towards the front line. These would be opened up in a zig-zag fashion to provide trenches for troops in no man's land, and also between the British and German trenches. On 30 June the Battalion marched from Bouzincourt to the front line in a good mood, confident of success in the upcoming advance, as many were.

1 July 1916 is a date now synonymous in Britain with the First World War, when thirteen British and six French Divisions went 'over the bags' against six German Divisions. On the 32nd Divisions flank, the 8th Division suffered severe losses and had to be relieved by the 12th Division almost immediately. The 32nd Division captured the Leipzig Redoubt, but not Thiepval which was the main objective, and would not be captured until 26 September. Casualties were very heavy – on the British side on 1 July alone there were nearly 60,000 casualties, with over 19,000 killed. If the NER Battalion had remained as an Infantry Battalion instead of being changed to a Pioneer Battalion, it is likely they would have lost heavily also on 1 July and their story would be very different.

The only sap that was able to be opened was Sanda sap, the Germans still holding the line in the other sap's areas. Sanda sap was soon clogged with dead and wounded men, but the German end had been blown in by a chance shell which helped C Company to open it. Sanda was fully opened at around 1700 but the Battalion struggled with the work of keeping this and the original communications open. This was due to wounded heading to the rear, whilst water and bomb carrying parties attempted to move to the front. A Company had little work to go and helped 218 Field Company Royal Engineers to repair wire and the British front line, and B Company carried water and bombs across no man's land to the Highland Light Infantry occupying the Leipzig Redoubt. D Company was held up by gas shelling and stood by until night fall when they were detailed to bury the dead. On 2 July C Company had managed to improve the communication lines and continued to do so until relieved by a company of the 6th Battalion South Wales Borderers on 4 July.

B Company spent several nights in the trenches until 3 July, coming under attack from shell fire and gas, whilst D Company worked on roads to improve access for motor ambulances. A Company was attached to the 12th Division on 5 July for carrying parties, and B and C Companies went into the front line on 9 July to relieve the North Hampshire Pioneers for a week, suffering gas attacks involving a new type that took around six hours to take effect. A and C Companies were later involved in making a prolonged tunnel towards the German lines, to emerge there when the German lines were captured, thus creating an instant communications line. Confusion came about when it was not realised if the line was already in British hands, or still German occupied. It was decided on the night of 13-14 July to keep the sap closed and have the Battalion Lewis gunners in position just in case the Germans broke through and used the tunnel against its makers.

The Battalion left the Somme on the evening of 16 July, moving to Loos a day later and arriving on 27 July. During the Battalions sixteen days on the Somme, ten Other Ranks were killed with eighty-three wounded, and one Officer missing with three wounded.

Loos and the remainder of 1916

Lieutenant Colonel Pears, commander of the Battalion, left the unit on 4 August for hospital, as he was suffering from cancer. He was aware he had it for a while but was determined to stay with the unit for as long as possible. Sadly he died later that year. For its time at Loos until the end of August the Battalion was attached to the 16th (Irish) Division. Whilst uneventful, the stay was not pleasant as they were surrounded on all three sides by the enemy, the ground often swept by machine gun fire. Attempts to camouflage any noise that may attract enemy fire included trying to muffle the noise of the horse drawn transport, which brought up supplies at night. During the time here the Battalion received unit markings in the form of transfers to be applied to the helmets to aid recognition. The design must have been impressive, as one wearer was stopped by two Generals who wished to inspect the fine art adorning his steel helmet.

C Company returned to the 32nd Division on 5 September to dig tunnels under no man's land, seeking instructions on how to do so as this was new territory for them. They were able to get advice and made a good job of the tunnel, however prior to their arrival the Germans were already aware of the existence of the tunnel. Day and night time raids were made on the British front line to destroy the tunnel, which often involved dropping 50lb bombs down the tunnel shaft. To deter attackers, the Battalion Lewis gunners were placed at posts guarding the shaft head entrances. The other three Companies re-joined 32nd Division during September, undertaking typical Pioneer Battalion work. D Company were also used to work on both light railways and standard gauge railways. During mid to late September the Battalion was moved around, occupying different points until quickly returning to the 32nd Division at the end of September. The surprising rapid return to the 32nd Division after moving away was later explained as it was believed there was due to be a German attack on the section of line held by 32nd Division.

On their return, the NER Battalion was designated a dedicated Railway Battalion under the Director of Railways. One of the lessons learnt from the Battle of the Somme was the need for improved transportation, and especially more use of the two foot light railways. Lieutenant Colonel Shakespear later remarked that "no better selection could have been made, for no Battalion of the British Army contained more railway experts". The irony of this was probably not lost on those who were aware of Geddes original approach to the War Office over two years previously, offering them a dedicated railway unit made of experienced railwaymen, which was declined.

On 27 September the Battalion left for Bethune, and entrained to Acheux where they were employed on railway work. For October the Headquarters and Battalion Transport stayed at Acheux Wood whilst the men would stay as close to their work as possible. The Battle of the Somme was still raging, and would do so until November. The men of the NER Battalion saw others coming back from the front festooned with souvenirs of the German Army, caps and helmets being especially popular. In late October and early November, A Company worked with the 119th Railway Company, Royal Engineers in working on a light railway over the old British and German front lines and towards the present front line. The closer to the front they got, the more German shells began to fall, which lead to one man of the NER Battalion remarking "I feel truly thankful I have not been offered the job of stationmaster"!

By mid-November the Battalion had completed the Aveluy to Mouquet Farm railway line, and then built a loop on the line from Courcelles to Hebuterne. They also constructed a siding at Maily-Maillet for a large railway gun, all of this work mostly done in conjunction with the 277th Railway Company, Royal Engineers. Similar work was done for the rest of the year, with Christmas Day being a day off with sports events held and men allowed into the local village. New Years' Day was similar, with no 'lights out' at night in camp.

1917

Two parties from B Company temporarily left the Battalion in mid-January 1917 – one of these contained seventy men under Second Lieutenant Jellicoe to work on the Railway Operating Division's standard gauge railway lines. The other party, again of seventy men and under Second Lieutenant Smith, were to work on the light railways for the 1st Army, behind Vimy Ridge. The work took both groups three weeks after which they returned to the Battalion.

A morale-lifting occasion on 11 February was the sudden arrival of sixteen bags of mail. Twenty-two letters and four parcels went to one man, with another receiving twenty-eight letters and three parcels – but still wanted more as he had a girl back home. By this time the Battalion was employed on building a Light Railway workshop, taking over from Royal Engineers who had undertaken some basic preliminary construction. The workshop was to take up 75,000 square feet, the parts arriving from England in sea-going barges which had crossed the English Channel then travelled up a canal to be moored and offloaded alongside the site. Fortunately the parts were numbered to aid in their erection. The workshop was designed to accommodate both narrow and standard gauge railways, and as well as the workshop itself, access roads, drainage, water supply and accommodation huts also had to be constructed. The work was completed on 31 March and handed over to a Mechanical Company of the Royal Engineers who would install and run the equipment of the workshop.

The NER Battalion then marched in blinding snow to Berguette, entraining for Poperinghe. Work commenced on the Great Midland Railway, a standard gauge railway starting two miles north of Poperinghe and heading east towards the Yser Canal. The ultimate destination of the railway depended on the success of the Ypres Salient offensives planned for that year. Each Company of the Battalion was responsible for a certain length of railway, each having one or two companies from an Infantry or Labour Battalion attached to aid with unskilled labour. A Company also had the job of erecting a timber pile bridge over the Poperinghe Canal, which had a water level twenty-two feet below the planned bridge level. This required a span of 120 feet, and the bridge was finished in just fourteen days.

The Yser canal was to be filled in to allow the crossing of the railway and tanks, but was in constant danger of shelling as the canal banks were under observation from the enemy just 1,800 yards away. Skilful and extensive use of camouflage avoided casualties, and the railway was completed on time by mid-June, the Battalion then being put onto light railway work. The light railway network in the area was already well developed but there were plans for a large extension of it owing to the forthcoming offensive. It would also require extending forward into captured territory once the attack started. In anticipation of this the Battalion was placed in the 18th Corps Light Railway Advance – this unit also included the 18th Battalion Northumberland Fusiliers as well as others, totalling 3,918 men of all ranks.

A training camp was set up where tips for laying light railways as quick as possible were shared, each unit having different preferred methods. The ultimate aim was to be able to lay the railway liens as quick as the infantry advanced over enemy ground, minimising the distance between the front line and the nearest railhead for supplies. The units would be engaged in carrying the light railway onwards from the Yser canal. Maps issued showed the intended alignment from the Yser Canal to the front line, and after that a blue line went towards St Julien and onwards to the edge of the map. All eventualities were planned for and many changes were made to the plans before the launch of the attack.

Zero hour for the attack, the Third Battle of Ypres, was at 0615 on 31 July. By 0800 there were already three hundred men working, well spread, to advance the light railways. The gap at the canal bank was widened by D Company fo the light railway to advance through. The first shift of men was relieved at noon, having suffered no heavy casualties. By midday on 1 August 500 yards of railway line had been finished, despite heavy rainfall creating awful conditions to work let alone fight in. A further 300 yards was receiving the final touches for completion and another 300 yards were close to completion. A single shell caused forty casualties mainly of the Pioneer Battalion of the Gloucestershire Regiment who were amongst the second shift of the day.

Work on the light railway continued until the end of August. During this time the camp for the men constantly moved, trying to avoid casualties to men moving from the camp to their place of work. On 30 August the line was over to the 7th Canadian Railway Troops, by which point the line was at Admiral's Farm, which a month prior was a position in the German lines. As well as the main railway, spurs had also been built to serve artillery batteries which moved closer to the German line. At one stage, one section of track was being laid per minute on a 900 yard spur leading up to a 6 inch Howitzer battery, whilst repair gangs were kept at the ready day and night. During this work the Battalion suffered casualties of seven men killed and sixty-two wounded.

After being relieved, the Battalion returned to the 32nd Division, travelling to Ghyvelde on the Belgian coast in a convoy of around forty double-deck motor buses. These buses had formerly been used on the streets of London, and after a number went to the Western

Front still in civilian colours during the Relief of Antwerp in 1914, more were requisitioned by the British Army. The busses, superb for troop transport, were militarised by being painted khaki, with the glass windows of the lower deck being removed, usually replaced with wooden boarding. The twenty-two mile journey in hot weather must have been pleasant for those with a seat on the upper deck of the open top buses.

At Ghyvelde the Battalion went into tented accommodation, and the day after arrival saw the men enjoy a much earned swim in the North Sea. On 10 September the Battalion marched to Nieuport, screening and repairing trenches whilst under fire, including from long-range German naval guns at Ostend. The canal was also drained with the canal lock being filled in. As the Lewis gunners had not had much work whilst the unit was on railway construction duties, at Nieuport they were put under the guidance of Lieutenant Sadler. Lieutenant Sadler was sent to a machine gun school for instruction on the latest tactics in the employment of machine guns, and also had the duty of ensuring nothing had been forgotten since the last time they were in action.

Otober saw the Battalion march to Adinkerke where they boarded barges in pouring rain, the men crammed in like sardines whilst wet through, spending the night aboard as the barges moved down the canal to Coudekerke, where the unit rested for a fortnight. The rest mainly involved the cleaning and polishing of uniforms, and burnishing the metal work on transport vehicles. After this was completed, the men were instructed to paint over all exposed metal parts on the vehicles, much to their chagrin.

After this period of rest the Battalion moved to Brielen, bringing them back into the Ypres area – the last few miles of the journey being over railway lines laid by the men a few months before. After leaving the train, the Battalion marches until stopped on a road near St Jean Station, and told they could camp on either side of the road. The initiative of the Pioneers meant it did not take long for suitable shelters to spring up – material being acquired from a nearby Royal Engineers Dump. The Battalion left 32nd Division and came under the instruction of the Chief Engineer of the 18th Corps to work on roads. The main task was to find where the road used to be between St Julien and Poelkapelle, and then to rebuild it. For the Pioneers who took pride in their work, this job was very unsatisfactory, the muddy conditions in this area hampering work. The attention of the Germans, shelling them during the day and bombing them from the air at night caused further discomfort to the men. After this the unit was employed on railway construction again, staying in the area working on the light railways. By now the light railway had reached St Julien and was being extended in other directions.

Christmas 1917 saw A Company beat a team from the Royal Flying Corps in a football match, winning 4-0. Christmas lunch for the Battalion consisted of meat pies, plum pudding, and two pints of beer per man. Each man was also issued with 150 cigarettes, fifty as a gift from the Battalion and the remaining hundred a gift from the North Eastern Railway. The original plan for the day was to have sports after lunch, however following the dinner no one appeared keen, and the sports were postponed until New Years' Day. The rest of the day was then spent resting, some taking the opportunity for a sleep, until a traditional Christmas dinner of Turkey. B Company were billeted separate to the rest of the Battalion, and at their location at Lancashire Farm had a football match with a local Royal Flying Corps Kite Balloon section. This was followed by a Christmas dinner of turkey and Yorkshire puddings. The Battalion was to spend three-and-a-half months in the Ypres area in total at this time, moving around various camps in the area as railway work required.

1918

The exit of Russia from the war in 1917 released large numbers of German troops for the Western Front, and it was common knowledge that a German offensive was expected. Rumours reached a crescendo in March that the attack was imminent – new defensive positions guns in old positions behind the lines seemed to confirm this. The German spring offensive started on 21 March – the Battalion was located north of the attack, so at first it was a quiet day for the unit. Once reports came in, orders came for the Battalion to stop work on lines east of the Yser canal and to wire a bridge ready for demolition. They were also ordered to dismantle railway sidings, dumps and yards, and salvage the material where possible to avoid it falling into enemy hands.

During late March whilst this work was going on, the Steenbeek

Bridge collapsed whilst a light railway train was crossing it, the Steenbeek at the time twice its normal width, washing away some of the bank underneath the bridge. The train was carrying a repair party including a platoon of the Battalion as well as Canadian troops, the locomotive and the first wagon of the train falling into the water. Rescue efforts by men of the Battalion saved all the men from the wagon, however sadly the driver and fireman were pinned under their locomotive and drowned.

On 13 April urgent orders came in for the Battalion to return to headquarters after lunch, from where they marched to Poperinghe and entrained. After detraining at midnight and marching for a mile, then detailing to sleep in a field in a road, the men awoke to find they were now attached to the 1st Australian Division, 15th Corps. They were to be employed in preparing defensive lines and strong points around La Motte and then Petit sec Bois, a line 4,000 yards long. This work took a week to do and involved a 'stand to' in the trenches from 0430 to 0530 each day, to prove the men's readiness in case of attack. Each Company was detailed an individual Infantry Battalion's front line to fortify if necessary. The Lewis gunners were also brought together for instruction under newly promoted Captain Sadler in preparation for their likely role. This work continued through May until the Battalion was transferred to the 18th Corps on 29 May, the unit being attached to the 52nd Division, arriving on 31 May. One Company worked on huts for the Divisional Headquarters for most of June while the rest of the Battalion worked on trenches at night time, getting there via light railway over Vimy Ridge.

There was still a very real threat of a further German advance, and there were designated positions for the Battalion to defend in case of attack. The end of June saw the Battalion go back to officially being a Pioneer Battalion again, losing its role as Railway Construction Battalion – one change this entailed was the loss of the unit's motor transport. Structural changes to the British Army as a whole meant that D Company was broken up in July, the men staying with the Battalion but distributd amongst the other three companies to bolster their numbers.

The Battalion entrained to Tangy on 23 July for a spell of rest, the first British troops to be billeted here since 1915. In early August the Battalion returned to work, still with the 52nd Division who were holding the south east portion of Vimy Ridge. The Battalion stayed in reserve, having an uneventful time apart from some night work on repairing trenches. In mid-August the Division was relieved which gave the Battalion several day's rest. By now the tide had turned on the Western Front – the German advance had come to a stop at the British forces started to advance. This began with the Battle of Amiens on 8 August, returning to the open warfare not experienced since 1914. Trenches were now far more temporary positions with advances over longer distances with the British Army effectively employing all arms – Tanks, air power, machine guns, grenades, rifle grenades and mortars, weapons and tactics introduced and improved to perfection over the past years. Aircraft strafed and bombed the Germans whilst Heavy Tanks accompanied by Infantry punched holes in the German front lines. Through these holes came the lighter, faster Medium Tanks and Armoured Cars who would cause havoc in the rear. The advances were followed up by the artillery, increasingly using motor transport to keep up.

On 21 August the 52nd Division was allotted to the 6th Corps of the 3rd Army, the Battalion following the main advance, the main objective being Gommecourt. One Company was employed in making an assembly trench in no man's land, and the other two improved artillery tracks. After August, the Battalion was used on road building, and unlike the unsatisfactory work in the Ypres Salient this was much more successful owing to fine weather and solid clay under the road. Rapid completion of the road meant that traffic could travel on it straight away. The very night the road was completed leading up to Bullecourt, ration and water carts were able to get right up to the front line to supply the men there. The next day heavy guns were moving up the road, towed by large Holt Caterpillar Tractors.

In September the Battalion Horse Transport suffered losses due to enemy aerial bombing – this included the deaths of some of the few remaining North Eastern Railway horses, given to the Battalion in 1914. The men went into the front line on 15 September, A and B Companies both working and manning trenches. Major Martin was killed on 17 September and Lieutenant McKay seriously wounded as a German shell landed nearby as they were on their way to inspect A Company's next job.

In preparation for the next advance, in late September three crossing were made by the Battalion across the dry Canal du Nord. It was necessary for the canal to be filled in and made suitable for crossing by artillery and vehicles. Once this was complete, three days were spent burying the dead and also reorganising. The start of October was spent building and repairing trenches, entraining for Vauix Vraucourt on the afternoon of 8 October. A six mile march to Manin followed where the Battalion was rested with a programme of parades and football until 15 October. For the rest of the month the Battalion worked under the Chief Engineer of 8th Corps. C Company went to Douai to work on bridges, and A and B Company went to Raches to work on roads.

On 4 November, with the Battalion back with the 52nd Division, the 1st, 3rd and 4th Armies advanced five miles on a thirty mile front between Sambre to Valenciennes. This included the double obstacle of the River Scheldt and the Jard Canal, the crossings facilitated by the NER Battalion along with other Pioneer Battalions and Royal Engineer Field Companies. The Battalion helped the advance to traverse heavily waterlogged areas, made difficult by the retreating enemy destroying all bridges and most culverts. Mines blown on roads also caused disruption to road transport and artillery which had to be repaired.

One bridge was found intact on 9 November, over the Antoing-Pommeroeul Canal, joyful locals helping the Battalion to repair the bridge and make it fit for heavy transport. The advance continued through November until 11 November, when the entire Division halted along the road from Nimy to Jurbrise at 1100. No official news of the Armistice reached the men until the next day. The celebrations of the war finally being over were followed by a period of supplies being short, and an irregular delivery of rations as the food was instead diverted to locals and refugees. The refugees streamed towards the British positions after their home towns and villages had been left bare by the retreating Germans. Work continued for the NER Battalion, having plenty to do it in cleaning up war damage, mostly filling in craters on roads and repairing bridges. Training filled in any spare time, bemusing many now that the war was supposed to be over. Despite the armistice, however, there was still no formal end of the state of war between Germany and the Allied powers, and this would remain so until the signing of the Treaty of Versailles on 28 June 1919.

On 26 November the Battalion assembled at Masnuy St Jean, a small village that could only just accommodate the Battalion, and here they had educational classes to prepare men for demobilisation and return to civilian life. Games, ceremonial parades, and an inter-company Divisional football tournament took pace in December.

1919

A Divisional parade on 18 January 1919 required much spit and polish for the men, with a second ceremony on 27 January when the Battalion was issued with its Kings Colours, a very proud moment for the men. The ceremony required many rehearsals beforehand, and also needed the services of a band from the Royal Scots as the Battalion did not have its own. The ceremony took place on ground with hard frozen snow, the Senior Chaplain dedicating the colours, after which Corps Commander Sir Arthur Godley presented to the colours to Captain E. R. Wilkinson. Sir Arthur Godley gave a speech, followed by Colonel King of the Battalion giving a brief account of the Battalion's History. After this, the Battalion formed in line, and as Captain Wilkinson raised the Colours, the Battalion presented arms and the band played the national anthem. The Colour party then took its post while the Battalion marched past the Corps Commander.

A period of games and easy exercise followed as well as a series of boxing matches as demobilisation went on. Men returned to Britain based on their length of service on also the grade of their peacetime job. Railwaymen were a high grade and so demobilisation was not slow for the NER Battalion. All training ceased in February owing to the low strength of the Battalion, and on 20 March the remnants of the Battalion went to Soignies, halfway between Mons and Brussels, with a cadre of just thirty men and three Officers. Colonel King left the Battalion for England at the beginning of June, then back to his peacetime post in Argentina.

Two weeks later the Battalion went to Antwerp where it boarded sea going barges down to Boulogne, then ordered to return to Newcastle. On the Battalion's return to Newcastle it was received by the Mayor and other civil dignitaries, and the men spent several days in Newcastle being entertained before going to Ripon where most of the cadre was demobilised. Captain Sadler, Captain Tindell, Corporal Train and Corporal Eldon were kept on and were to go to Aintree to receive the Battalion Transport and equipment which arrived two weeks later from the port of Richborough. At Aintree it was handed over to the Ordnance and the four men returned to Newcastle again with the Battalion Colours. They were met at Newcastle by the Divisional Goods Manager of the North Eastern Railway, C. A. Lambert and his assistant, as well as other local NER Officials. In addition they were joined by Major Cole and several other old Officers of the Battalion. The party then marches to the Cathedral Church of St Nicholas where many men from the Battalion had gathered, having been given special leave by the North Eastern Railway for the occasion.

After a service, the Colours were deposited in a place of honour. The next day, the four remaining men of the Battalion went to Ripon for demobilisation – and the 17th (North Eastern Railway) Battalion Northumberland Fusiliers, ceased to exist. Despite the unit ceasing to exist, and the demobilisation of the men, many of the men reserved on Z Reserve in case of Germany resuming hostilities, however this was abolished on 31 March 1920.

During the war, the four Officers and sixty-three Other Ranks of the NER Battalion were killed, a further thirty-eight Other Ranks dying from wounds, four dying from gas and three dying of sickness, as well as Lieutenant Colonel Pears dying of cancer in England. A more complete history of the Battalion can be found in Lieutenant Colonel Shakespear's account of 1919, with a foreword by Field Marshal Haig and an introduction by Sir E. C. Geddes.

32nd Battalion Northumberland Fusiliers

With the formation of the 17th Battalion Northumberland Fusiliers, which comprised of four Companies, a further two additional Reserve companies were created, E and F. When the remainder of the Battalion went to Catterick in June 1915, the Resserve Companies stayed behind at Hull until 24 July when they moved by train to Cramlington, joining the Reserve Companies of the 16th, 18th and 19th Battalions of the Northumberland Fusiliers. These were all amalgamated in August to form the 28th Battalion Northumberland Fusiliers, and at the end of August moved to Bardon Moor. Here the 28th Battalion split, the original E and F Companies of the NER Battalion forming the

32nd Battalion Northumberland Fusiliers. Late summer and autumn was spent at Bardon Moor, and then moved into huts at Ripon in November. A move was made to Harrogate on 22 December with the men billeted in houses and hotels.

In February 1916 the 32nd Battalion moved to Newcastle, billeting in schools and other buildings. As well as training, the men would also undertake guard duties in the local area. May saw the men move to Usworth, the men now sleeping in tents, with intensive training undertaken to prepare replacements for the NER Battalion now that it was on the Western Front. Once men started leaving for the front, the Battalion was later changed to become the 80th Trainign Reserve Battalion, and recruits who were not North Eastern Railway men were enrolled for the first time. The Battalion was disbanded around Christmas 1917, however by this time it was highly doubtful that any of the original 32nd Battalion men from the North Eastern Railway men were still in the unit.

The Darlington National Projectile Factory

The North Eastern Railway Shell Shop, or the Darlington National Projectile Factory as it was officially known, was fully opened in late 1915 on the Darlington North Road Works site. The 'shell shop' as it became universally known, was built by the Government, but run by the North Eastern Railway on the proviso that after the war the building and all the specialist machinery inside would be transferred to the NER. The shell shop was powered by electricity throughout, and employed 150 men and 1,000 women at any one time, working in three sets of eight hour shifts per day, ensuring twenty-four hour operation, with a single half-hour meal break halfway through the shift. In total the women employed at the shell shop worked forty-five hours a week, working six out of seven days. The opening of munitions factories throughout Britain during the war brought vast numbers of women into the workplace, many for the first time, giving them useful skills and wages which without the war they would never have experienced. Whilst the women employed in nursing and driving motor vehicles (usually ambulances) behind the battlefields tended to be from the middle and upper classes, those employed at munitions factories were predominantly working class.

In common with factories of the period, the importance of time management was strongly impressed on the workers with penalties for getting to work late. Article five of the 'Rules and Regulations to be observed by women in the shell shop, Darlington loco works', issued 10 March 1916 by Chief Mechanical Engineer Vincent L. Raven, stated that "any woman not having obtained her check at the time appointed may come in not more than fifteen minutes afterwards but will lose half an hour. Women are expected to be in their places ready for work when the bell is rung for commencing", and the tail end of article six said how "bad time-keeping will be held sufficient reason for dispensing with a woman's services". Despite these seemingly draconian rules which may give the impression of laziness of the workforce, in reality the 'munitionettes' were very good timekeepers and superb workers, often being complimented for doing the work as well as, if not better than their male counterparts. This enthusiasm comes not only to help with the war effort, but also due to the wages and subsequent lifestyle which work in munitions factories gave them, such as freedom they had never experienced before. One person wrote in 1918, "to-day (a woman) may smoke, she may wear trousers, she may crop her hair short, she may live alone in flats, she may walk in the streets in khaki and salute other khaki-clad beings, for all the world as if she were a man". How successful the rules and regulations were in deterring poor attendance is impossible to gauge, but at any rate the attendance rate of the munitionettes was impeccable. According to an article on the factory in the May 1916 issue of the *North Eastern Railway Magazine*, "the record being so good as to make it difficult to express the loss of time as a percentage". Despite the initial administrative problems faced by the North Eastern Railway in dealing with the traffic to the factory at first, and then later both to and from the factory, before long it just became another part of North Eastern Railway life and "even the Boy Scouts, in their fearsome uniform, who act as messengers for the Shell Factory, are regarded with indifference. We have always the satisfaction of feeling that any additional labour we are called upon to undertake is forming some little part of the great endeavour of the Allies to defeat the common enemy – Germany and her supporting countries".

The 'shell shop' did not deal with the explosives, just making the shells themselves, which meant the workers here avoided the dangers of TNT poisoning. This could lead to the skin turning yellow and even death, as well as the risk of an explosion which occurred to other munitions works during the war. The worst accident had been at Chilwell in Nottinghamshire on 1 July 1918, killing 134 (of these only thirty two could be identified) and injuring 250 more. This did not necessarily mean it was the safest occupation – fast, heavy machinery still had the ability to maim or kill its operator with ease. Eye injuries were particularly common for those who worked with lathes, and a woman's long hair could get caught in a machine, scalping her leading to serious injury or even death. Although a 'mop' cap was worn, these were not always worn correctly, and hair could come out from underneath.

Despite the dangers, the benefits of working in the munitions factories far outweighed the negatives. In addition it gave women the ability take as much a part in the war effort as the men and the vast majority were now given exposure to an entirely new world of freedom. By April 1918, the average wage for women working in national projectile factories was £2 3s 4d a week, and although this was well below the male average of £4 14s 18d a week, women were still earning more than ever before, especially as many had not had paying jobs until the war. It was now more acceptable for women to live on their own or with other women, and they would frequently be seen socialising in numbers in public, going to the theatre or cinema together, or even to the pub, a traditionally male location. Despite claims that the affluent munitions workers were getting drunk, the women would need to have drunk more pints to become intoxicated owing to the diluted beer which was being served during the war. Its strength being summed up in a popular song composed in 1915:

> Lloyd George's Beer, Lloyd George's Beer,
> In the brewery, there's nothing doing,
> All the waterworks are brewing!

Another verse going:

> Dip your bread in it, shove your head in it
> From January to October,
> And I'll bet a penny that you'll still be sober.

Many munitions factories also organised social activities in-house, with sports clubs springing up for football, hockey and netball. Football was especially popular, and was strongly associated with the working classes where the majority of the women workers came from. The Darlington 'shell shop' had its own team, and if men thought women wearing trousers was racey enough, they would have been even more shocked to see the women footballers in their shorts and bare knees, looking much like their male counterparts apart from a longer shirt and a cap. The munitions team played other women's football teams across the area – the name however seemed to change frequently, being known as the 'Darlington Munitionettes', 'NER Munition Girls', 'Darlington Railway Athletic' and others. Whilst under the name of the NER Munitionettes the team played a male team of soldiers recuperating from injuries at the VAD Hospital in Darlington on 6 October 1917 at Feetham.

The 'shell shop' was mainly employed in producing shells for the 18 pounder field gun – the most numerous artillery piece of the British Army during the war, and the main weapon of the Royal Field Artillery alongside the 4.5 inch howitzer. By the end of the war, the Darlington National Projectile Factory had produced 1,064,665 18 pounder shrapnel shells which, from the shell casing, projected small lead balls, devastating against men and horses on open ground, and 428,435 18 pounder high explosive shells. In smaller numbers there were also 134,876 6 inch high explosive shells produced, as well as 20,000 4 inch heavy naval practice shot. In addition to manufacturing new shells, the brass cartridge cases, which contained the propellant to fire the shells on quick-firing guns such as the 18 pounder and 4.5 inch howitzer, were brought back from the front and repaired to be used again. In total 1,864,447 18 pounder and 257,168 4.5 inch howitzer cartridge cases were repaired for re-use. In order to repair them, a scleroscope – a device used to measure the rebound hardness of an object – was used to look for any weaknesses or cracks in the casing unseen by the human eye. There was also the use of annealing, where brass is heated and then cooled to prevent new cracks forming when fired again. Brass shell cases that were either manufactured or repaired at the Darlington 'Shell Shop' can be identified by the 'E.RY' stamping on the bottom of the shell casing. In conjunction with the Telegraph Department at York, which employed around twenty women for the role, 775,000 fired percussion primers were repaired and made ready for filling elsewhere and used again.

After the war, as originally agreed upon by the Government, the factory became part of the Darlington Locomotive Works, along with any of the lathes, tools and other specialist machinery that the North Eastern Railway would find useful for making peacetime locomotives instead of wartime shells.

War Manufacture

The construction at short notice of a railway gun carriage for the coastal defence 9.2 inch gun as detailed in the chapter 'Outbreak' was just the tip of the iceberg. Although the dedicated munitions works was built at Darlington, the war was to see railway workshops around the country make all manner of interesting and unusual equipment for the war effort in all shapes and sizes. Some of the difficulties faced by the more esoteric equipment are mentioned by George Heppell, the Chief Draughtsman, when the North Eastern Railway was asked to produce horse-drawn water carts for the Army:

> The Government Department sent a full set of drawings to work to and I had to go to King's Cross to see one complete. There were several details I knew we could not make for want of special machines. I told Mr Raven what I thought and he said I had to send copies of the drawings to Gateshead Works and they would build the 47 carts. I had a lot of trouble and running about before I secured the plates for the water tanks as they were round and took a large plate which was very thin. At last I found a firm that could supply them. Then I had a lot of trouble in getting them galvanized after the tanks were finished. While they were being built Mr Bell, Manager at Gateshead Works, and I were sent to Woolwich Arsenal to see a tank complete in every detail. We had a letter of introduction to the General Manager from Mr Raven. When we found him he said he was very sorry but all the carts had gone. I asked him if he was sure and he went and enquired and said it was true all the carts had left

the works. I knew this was not true as I asked the guide in going to the office if any water carts were in the works and he said they were standing finished. After thanking the manager for his kindness and leaving him I got the guide to take us to them and found they were testing one so that we got all the information we required. The next difficulty was to get the details. I went to Manchester to see if any firm would make them. They were all full up. At last the G.E.R. fitted up a shop and supplied all the details. The next job was kitchen cookers. We soon built all we were asked to do in that line…

The horse-drawn vehicles were built by the Carriage and Wagon shops of the North Eastern Railway at York. Other horse-drawn vehicles built included 984 General Service Wagons which were the backbone of the Army Service Corps, Officers' Mess Carts and General Service Limbers, which were more manoeuvrable and could travel faster than the GS Wagons. These were made up out of two limbers joined together rather than one wagon body and in total, 412 of these 'covered goods and Special wagons for overseas' were built. Interestingly, some of the photographs showing the vehicles fresh from the works show them already marked up for use by the North Eastern Railway Battalion – the 17th (Pioneer) Battalion, Northumberland Fusiliers.

Also built at York were 400 20-ton covered wagons for use on French railways. York also made 1,850 stretchers, entrenching tools, pack saddles for artillery horses, and 400 clarifying reels for water tanks, to help purify the water taken up by the carts and then either drunk by or used for cooking for the troops. The Red Cross ambulance train consisting of sixteen carriages and the train of eight carriages built for the Director-General of Transportation were also York products.

Following the combat debut of the tank on 15 September 1916, the North Eastern Railway along with other railway companies received orders to make wagons capable of carrying the 28 ton metal monsters. In development since 1915, the prototype Mk 1 Tank was built in January 1916, and the introduction to combat of forty-nine of these in just nine months, and in complete secrecy, is testament to the hard work of those involved in the design and construction of the revolutionary new weapon. Although they had what is now viewed as a disappointing start, the tank was here to stay. Of the forty-nine tanks due to be involved, thirty-two reached their starting positions for the battle and of them, twenty-five went into action following the mechanical breakdown of the others. As well as increased production of the machines themselves, specialised, strengthened railway wagons had to be built to cope with the weight (just under thirty tons) concentrated on a very small surface area owing to the shape of the vehicle. Initially, existing flat wagons were used but these were far from ideal. They could only be loaded from the end and were not strong enough to cope with the tanks driving along a number of them, so could only be loaded and added to a train one at a time. This was much more time consuming than having the train of wagons set up and loaded in one go. Not only this, but structural failure was also a possibility when using vehicles not designed for the specific role and previously used where weights were spread more evenly. The newly designed 35 ton wagons, known as RECTANKS (REC coming from 'Railway Executive Committee') could be loaded from the side also, or if necessary a tank could be driven along a line of the wagons as they were strengthened to be able to deal with the weight. In all, forty of these were built by the NER at the York Carriage & Wagon Works, along with others built by the Midland Railway at Derby, the Lancashire & Yorkshire Railway at Horwich, and the Great Western Railway at Swindon. The design was so successful that it was kept in use and production with little change throughout the Second World War and beyond.

The Shildon wagon works were also put to good use – producing 118,936 nose caps for 6 inch High Explosive shells, 7,402 nose caps for 210 mm shells, 25,000 diaphragms for 18 pounders and 21,750 diaphragm discs. The measurement of 210 mm may be a mistake meaning 8 inch shells, as 210 mm is actually 8.25 inches. The British did not use 210 mm artillery in the First World War.

Gun carriages for enormous artillery pieces were constructed by the North Eastern Railway at Darlington. Fifteen complete carriages were built for early 8 inch howitzers, which used old Royal Navy warship guns bored out and shortened, and twenty-nine for long range 6 inch guns. Eighty-four carriages and 136 base plates were built for 10 inch bomb throwers (used against submarines and fitted on warships), along with twenty-three carriages for 4 inch P IX mountings (for naval use). In addition 100 plate racers for 3 inch guns (likely anti-aircraft) and twenty pedestals used for anti-aircraft 13 pounder guns (which would include the 13 pounder 9 cwt, 18 pounder guns relined to take a 13 pounder shell), which were fitted to motor lorries and used in Britain as well as on the various fronts. Finally platforms and pedestals for six pounder Hotchkiss guns were built.

Vast numbers of other miscellaneous items were produced at Darlington; 38,058 rifle parts, 460 axle trees for 4.5 inch howitzers (for which 8,634 various parts had also been made at Darlington and Gateshead) and 15,460 parts for 18 pounder guns. In late 1918 a heavy road trolley was produced, weighing eleven tons but capable of carrying fifty tons and to be hauled by one or more steam traction engines and designed to carry 'Yarrow' type marine boilers for use on ships, but it could be utilised for other purposes. A photograph of it exists showing it fully loaded and requiring two steam traction engines.

Gateshead was also heavily involved and 250 barrels were made there for 6 inch Newton trench mortars, 4 feet and 9 inches long and firing a 52 pound bomb. Also manufactured were 84 sets of gear for bow defence fittings for armed trawlers, 7,476 track lines for tanks, 1,150 brass wheel hubs for artillery wheels.

Whilst seventeen NER motor vehicles had been requisitioned, before he was appointed to the Ministry of Munitions, Chief Mechanical Engineer Vincent Raven was also interested in the possibility of building motor lorries for the Army. In fact Raven had gone so far as to promise Sir George Gibb (former General Manager of the North Eastern Railway and now on the Army Council) that they would build eighteen a week, similar to the Leyland three ton design. Chief Draughtsman Heppell told Raven he did not think it could be done, so Raven:

> sent for Mr Lockyer, Manager of the Works, and let him see the design of the lorry. He also told him that it could not be done as all the machines were running all the hours that God sent. However, he did not believe him and went over to the works to see if the machines were working as Mr Lockyer had said. He found two lathes standing for a few minutes. That was enough; he was more determined on building them than ever. After having a long talk with him I suggested that we should go to Preston and see Leyland's Works. He agreed and we went and saw Mr Leyland who took us around and pointed out that they had <u>600</u> special machines and could only turn out <u>7</u> Lorries per week. Nothing more was said after that.

The sheer numbers and variety of equipment produced by the North Eastern Railway shows the adaptability of the railways in the First World War to cater for the needs of modern warfare. Aside from all the equipment already mentioned, were also, in the words of the *North Eastern Railway Magazine*, "such things as picketing pegs and posts, mine-sinker parts, &c., but it is sufficiently comprehensive to prove that great railway companies are able not merely to carry the productions of others, but themselves to produce 'the goods'."

Wells-Hood

Wells-Hood's armoured antics first became known to the men of the North Eastern Railway when this note was published in the October 1914 edition of the *North Eastern Railway Magazine*:

> Mr Hood, who, as stated above, has received a commission in the Royal Marines, is in charge of a number of armoured motor cars which are manned by crack shots from the marines and work in conjunction with a cavalry regiment. The cars are proving very useful in making reconnaissances, and are a source of terror to the bands of Uhlans which infest the northern portion of the western battlefield.

The 'Uhlans' referred to were a German cavalry unit equipped with lances, however it quickly became a generic term for all German cavalry units.

William Wells-Hood was born in 1880 and had been a member on the North Eastern Railway staff since 1896 as an apprentice at York Locomotive Works, leaving for service in the Second Boer War but returning in 1901, again in the Locomotive Department. In 1904 he became Inspector of East Coast Trains, and on 10 January 1907 was made head of the North Eastern Railway Road Motor Department, sometime after moving to a position in the Passenger Department at York. After war broke out, he was freed for service and joined the Royal Naval Air Service in September 1914 as an Officer, holding the rank of sub-Lieutenant, and with his previous experience of motor vehicles was posted with the new Royal Naval Air Service's Armoured

Car Division in Belgium. This unit began by using the personal motor cars of the Officers of the Royal Naval Air Service, with armed men, to rescue downed pilots at a time when it was still open warfare on the Western Front. This developed into cars with more and more armour and equipped with machine guns not just used to rescue pilots but also to make raids on the enemy and used for scouting purposes. The cars used became relatively standardised using identical bodies on Rolls Royce, Wolseley or Talbot car chassis. A photograph that appeared in the December 1914 *North Eastern Railway Magazine* shows (by now) Lieutenant Wells-Hood in a Talbot armoured car. This was an improved design updated from the original armoured cars which had armoured bodies but the top, apart from a small protective position for the driver's upper body, was open. This improved type of Talbot had a larger superstructure and could also be fitted with two Maxim machine guns instead of the usual one. Wells-Hood described the cars as weighing 2 tons 12 cwt fully loaded with driver, machine guns and petrol, the armour alone weighing between 10 and 12 cwt. By late 1914 trench warfare had set in on the Western Front and opportunities for using the armoured cars were rapidly decreasing. Wells-Hood wrote:

> The wait we are having just now cannot be avoided, as all the armoured cars in the country are practically idle. This will be readily understood seeing the two forces have taken up position at such close quarters. We are all right for patrols, but this is not necessary now. We are also very good for making it uncomfortable for retreating enemy or covering cavalry.

In the same issue as the news of Wells-Hood's exploits were first published, a poem was included, with Wells-Hood in mind, being taken from *The Autocar* magazine and referring to the armoured cars such as Wells-Hood was using, from the viewpoint of a new car which was sent to the Western Front to be fitted with armour:

> I was all for speed when I came to the front
> And they wrapped me up in steel
> And sent me forward to bear the brunt
> To taste the joys of the Uhlan hunt
> With a dare-devil hand at the wheel.

Wells-Hood came across a former colleague whilst in Belgium – a North Eastern Railway motor vehicle driver called Stevenson was serving with the Royal Flying Corps driving a Dennis lorry when Wells-Hood bumped into him whilst on a walk in Bailleul after dinner. The lack of activity gave Wells-Hood and his fellow Officers opportunity to explore Belgium, in one trip covering around 140 miles, and claimed to know "every inch of the country between Nieuport and Armentieres". The occasional opportunity for action came with one of the gun lorries, again developed in Belgium, that were used as mobile artillery for the armoured cars, which were used at night time to a prepared position where they would fire on a pre-designated target before withdrawing:

> On November 20, we took a gun wagon to Nieuport and shelled a small village called Lenbertzde (this is likely to be a spelling mistake, probably meaning Lombartzyde). We fired over 40 shots – 3-lb. shells. We had no sooner moved away than the Germans put a shell on the identical spot where we had been standing....

The gun lorries, fitted with a 3 pounder gun, were initially made from the London B type double deck buses which were shipped to the Western Front still in civilian colours including destination blinds and with adverts for rapid troop transport in the defence of Antwerp.

The next day, Wells-Hood experienced a flight over the lines, planned to be from Nieuport to Ypres. Wells-Hood was armed with a rifle in case an enemy aircraft should show up, well wrapped up for a winter flight at 6,000 feet, however the flight was curtailed before reaching Ypres owing to engine trouble. Wells-Hood and his unit returned to England in December owing to the lack of work on the front for them. At the Royal Naval Air Service's Armoured Car Division's base at Wormwood Scrubs at the Talbot Works, they were re-equipped with the new Rolls Royce armoured cars. These were possibly the finest armoured car design, a major improvement on the previous designs. They were fully armoured with opening flaps over key areas such as the driver's position and the radiator which could be closed in action and opened when not to allow cooling for the engine and better visibility for the driver. In addition there was a revolving turret above the driver with a Maxim or Vickers machine gun. By 1915 the typical make up of an Armoured Car Squadron would be:

12 armoured cars (Rolls Royce or Lanchesters)

3 Seabrook armoured lorries (again, an improvement on those used in 1914, fully armoured with a 3 pounder gun and up to four Maxim machine guns)

6 supply lorries, usually Talbots

1 wireless lorry, usually a Wolseley

1 ambulance, usually a Wolseley

1 staff car

1 heavy lorry

36 motorcycles – these would be used for scouting and communication, although some had a sidecar which were fitted again with a Maxim or Vickers machine gun, which could be dismounted from the sidecar. The motorcycle and sidecars were usually Scott machines, and the solo motorcycles usually made by Douglas.

March 1915 saw Wells-Hood and his Squadron depart for German South-West Africa. At the start of the war, German forces had overrun British territory, and threatened to invade South Africa. It was thought prudent to rid the Germans from here, as the possibility of an attack on South Africa meant 50,000 soldiers were tied up here when they could be used in more important theatres of war. The terrain here was much more suited for armoured cars, and 1 Squadron arrived at Walfisch Bay on 16 April with Wells-Hood amongst 122 men of the squadron. At first, the armoured cars had to be transported by rail twenty-two miles to Swakopmund as the road in-between was soft sand, the journey taking five hours in very hot weather. Arriving at Swakopmund Wells-Hood surveyed part of the railway using a petrol powered inspection trolley with a maximum speed of thirty miles per hour for ten miles, the trolley being light enough to be lifted up by four strong men – this reminded him of the North Eastern Railway's petrol railcar used for inspections back in Britain. From Swakopmund they drove the armoured cars inland, but still faced difficulties owing to sand. On 26 April he saw action for the first time in the campaign, where a force of mounted German troops approached the front line, dismounted from their horses and then advanced. The armoured cars "did good work. It was a sharp little action, the Germans losing their Officer commanding, two officers and six men, whilst we found fifteen wounded and took eighteen prisoners. I got a cut on my head about 1½ inches long but quite superficial. This was done, I think, by the case of a bullet that made its way into the car. It is only a scratch."

It is not clear from Wells-Hood's letter which action this refers to, but it appears to be the battle at Trekkopjes, which involved nine armoured cars, and was the first battle of the campaign. Following this battle, 1 Squadron advanced with the soldiers, pushing the German forces northwards, particularly guarding the railway. Although the terrain was more suited to armoured cars and other motor vehicles than the Western Front, there were still difficulties and the railway was the only effective way of transporting supplies. The terrain varied from soft sand to heavy and sharp rocks which barred progress or damaged tyres, as well as high daytime temperatures and below freezing night time temperatures. Trekkopjes was the main battle of the campaign, but some use was found for the armoured cars at night, driving up to German positions, the quiet Rolls Royce engines making them almost undetectable, then when in position turning the headlights on and opening fire with the machine guns before withdrawing, harassing and unnerving an enemy already being constantly chased by the British forces. The German forces surrendered on 8 July 1915, and Wells-Hood returned to England.

On 1 December 1915 he was on a ship bound for Kola in Russia, to assist the Russian forces in fighting the Germans there. This unit was the Russian Armoured Car Division, made up from 15 and 17 Squadrons of the Royal Naval Armoured Car Division, mostly equipped with 33 Lanchester armoured cars. These had a similar turreted body to the Rolls Royce cars but on a different chassis. There was also one Rolls Royce, and several Pierce-Arrow armoured lorries. They were later reinforced with an additional Rolls Royce and nine armoured Ford Model Ts. They were not able to land at Kola owing to ice covering the sea so offloaded at Alexandrovsk, where a railway line was being built between Petrograd and Kola. With Kola closed to shipping, the only way to get materials to Kola from Alexandrovsk was via sledge, and Wells-Hood used his expertise to help develop a sledge route; his assistance in the construction of the line earned Wells-Hood the Russian Order of St Anne.

When summer finally came, the few hours of sunshine per day being changed for sunlight all through the night, Wells-Hood and his unit were able to proceed south across Russia, on a 5 feet gauge railway line (compared with the standard gauge, used in Britain and many other places, of 4 feet and 8½ inches). Wells-Hood took much interest in the line, especially from an engineering viewpoint as it had been changed from the previous gauge of 3 feet and 6 inches, which would have entailed massive issues, including replacement of bridges to take the wider rails, locomotives and rolling stock, however after enquiries he was told that the changeover was done without any closure of the line. Also of interest was the fact that the locomotives burned wood, not coal. When the train reached the first town, the British were met with much enthusiasm from the local population, around 1,000 crowding the station, as well as the Mayor and twenty Officers being on hand to greet them. After this they were taken to a dinner at a local hotel in horse-drawn carriages, which may sound very enjoyable but as Wells-Hood reported, "as the vehicles had been built in the last century, and the streets were paved with cobble stones, the journey was not one of unalloyed delight". The dinner met the approval of all though, despite some *faux pas* caused by cultural differences beforehand – one Lieutenant after shaking the hands of nearly a dozen Officers festooned with medals and other decorations, came across a man in black who bowed and held his hand out – the Lieutenant gave him his hat, thinking he was a waiter, which the man then put on a peg – it transpired when they all sat at the dinner table that this 'waiter' was actually the Lord Mayor! After this, the train proceeded further south until they reached Moscow, experiencing "real rain" for the first time in around six months, with flowers and fauna in bloom, a welcome change from the snow, ice and accompanying freezing temperatures they had first experienced. They were again greeted with much enthusiasm in Moscow, being entertained for several days, comparing it to a "York military Sunday". After a highly enjoyable stay here, the train moved further south, passing through the Cossack district then through to the Caucasus, stopping at Vladikavkazand where they were entertained by Cossacks on their arrival, their dancing and knife skills impressing the men. From here the journey was to be made by armoured car. The vehicles were unloaded and prepared for the long journey, and then driven to Tiflis in Georgia then onwards to Sarokomish, where the armoured cars were inspected by the Grand Duke Nicholas of Russia. They then headed into Turkish Asia, fighting here for two months against the Turks and then returned to Romania by train. In Romania, they were to fight the Germans, Turkish and Austro-Hungarians who were advancing against the retreating Romanians. The armoured cars were often used to try and check the infantry advance, at least long enough until the enemy artillery was put in position and opened fire, which the armoured cars could not fight against.

Winter again stopped armoured car actions and they were put into storage whilst the men fought in the trenches alongside the Russians. Their allies, however, were losing the will to fight – the Russian Revolution was now months away and the hostility of Russian soldiers was caused almost as many problems as the enemy. This came to a head in Christmas 1917 when the men of the Division were held prisoner by their former allies. They were later released, and by March 1918 Wells-Hood was back in Britain on leave. With the formation of the Royal Air Force on 1 April 1918, Wells-Hood instead decided to be transferred to the British Army, staying with armoured cars, for apart from the Russian Division, the Royal Navy armoured cars had been transferred to the army back in 1915. Wells-Hood was made a Major and went to Mesopotamia with Rolls Royce armoured cars. He served here until the end of the war, returning to the North Eastern Railway after demobilisation and serving on the railway until his retirement.

Wells-Hood seemed to be a rather modest man despite his exciting exploits during the war, but during a lecture to the York Railway Lecture & Debating Society he did give a fascinating insight into armoured car operations of the First World War:

Imagine yourself one of four men inside an iron chamber four feet six inches in diameter, about the size of a section of a locomotive boiler turned on its end, and only four feet six inches high, covered in at the top, with a narrow slit six inches by three quarters of an inch in front for the driver to see through, and a small round hole for the gun – a pretty dark and gloomy place. You pass your own trenches and begin to hear the shriek and bursting of shells – in thirty seconds more the bullets begin to tap-tap on the armour plate; another thirty seconds and your gunner shouts 'enemy in sight', but you think you can do more damage a little further on. The shell bursts get louder and closer, the tap-tap of the bullets now becomes a pattering like steady rain. You are now within one hundred yards of the enemy's trenches and this time allow the gunners to open fire.

From now on you might as well be dumb, nothing can be heard

except the roar of your own Maxim, and a continual cascade of hot, empty cartridge cases is pouring out from the back of the gun, burning your bare knees and hands. You open a slide on the side of the car and have a momentary peep through a small inch-and-a-half hole, seeing a place where the enemy are more exposed to fire. Seizing the gunner's leg he ceases fire and you shout 'target left flank'. The turret is swung round and while doing this a sudden shock and vibration of the car draws the remark from the driver 'that was a near one, Sir'. The renewed roar of your own gunfire makes any reply useless. The second gunner now points to the ammunition behind you, and while you are handing the box containing the live belts to him, another nasty jar makes the driver look at you enquiringly. You motion to him to move the car backwards and forwards more quickly as the case may be. The enemy has picked up your range and are making good shooting. After twenty minutes, which seems like five, you find the ammunition getting low and the enemy's fire too hot, so you signal to the driver to run out of action.

The tidy car you started with is now a mass of empty ammunition boxes, lids and empty belts. Empty cartridge cases in thousands cover your legs. The car swerves to dodge the shell-holes on the track, and soon a cheer outside tells you that you are passing your own trenches, and in four minutes you are at Headquarters. You crawl out through the litter and mop your dirty hands, whilst a gunner hunts out your cap from amongst the empty cartridge cases, before you go in to make your report to the General. He greets you warmly and thanks you.

Bibliography

The following publications have been of great use in writing this book, as well as other sources listed below.

The North Eastern Railway Magazine bound volume 1912
The North Eastern Railway Magazine bound volume 1913
The North Eastern Railway Magazine bound volume 1914
The North Eastern Railway Magazine bound volume 1915
The North Eastern Railway Magazine bound volume 1916
The North Eastern Railway Magazine bound volume 1917
The North Eastern Railway Magazine bound volume 1918
The North Eastern Railway Magazine bound volume 1919
The North Eastern Railway Magazine bound volume 1920
North Eastern Express – The Journal of the North Eastern Railway Association, Anthology Number 1 – "Engines for France" by 'Progress' (aka Percy Rosewarne)
North Eastern Express – The Journal of the North Eastern Railway Association edition no 191 – "From the Railways to the Front" by Martin Bashforth
An Illustrated History of NER Locomotives, Ken Hoole, published by Oxford Publishing Co., 1988
North Eastern Railway Buses, Lorries & Autocars, Ken Hoole, published by Nidd Valley Narrow Gauge Railways Ltd, 1969
Locomotives of the North Eastern Railway, O.S. Nock, published by Littlehampton Book Services, 1974
The North Eastern Railway, Cecil J. Allen, published by Ian Allan Ltd, 1964

Twenty-Five Years of the North Eastern Railway 1898-1922, R. Bell,
  published by The Railway Gazette, 1951
British Railways and the Great War Volume 1, Edwin A. Pratt,
  published by Selwyn & Blount, 1921
British Railways and the Great War Volume 2, Edwin A Pratt,
  published by Selwyn & Blount, 1921
Sir Vincent Raven and the North Eastern Railway, Peter Grafton,
  published by Oakwood Press, 2005
North Eastern Record Volume 3, J. M. Fleming, published by The
  Historical Model Railway Society, 2000
Shildon-Newport In Retrospect, K. C. Appleby, published by The
  Railway Correspondence and Travel Society, 2008
*Durham Pals – 18ᵗʰ, 19ᵗʰ & 22ⁿᵈ Battalions of The Durham Light
  Infantry in the Great War*, John Sheen, published by Pen & Sword,
  2007
North Eastern Locomotives: A Draughtsman's Life, George Heppell,
  published by the North Eastern Railway Association, 2012
The Electric Locomotives of the North Eastern Railway, Ken Hoole,
  published by Oakwood Press, 1988
The 4-4-0 Classes of the North Eastern Railway, Ken Hoole,
  published by Ian Allan, 1979
Talbot in the First World War, Stephen Lally & John Tomsett,
  published by the Sunbeam Talbot Darracq Register, 2008
North Eastern Railway Roll of Honour, 1919
The Home Front in the Great War, David Bilton, published by Pen &
  Sword, 2004
*A Record of the 17ᵗʰ and 32ⁿᵈ Battalions Northumberland Fusiliers
  1914-1919 (NER) Pioneers*, Lt-Col Shakespear, published by
  Naval & Military Press, 2009
On Her Their Lives Depend: Munitions Workers in the Great War,
  Angela Woollacott, published by University of California Press, 1994
War Cars: British Armoured Cars in the First World War, David
  Fletcher, published by Stationery Office Books, 1987
*The Baby Killers: German Air Raids on Britain in the First World
  War*, Thomas Fegan, published by Pen & Sword, 2002
Other sources;
JFM7236 – Visiting of Dependents of Men on Active Service, John F,
  Mallon Collection

JFM7284/1 – Damage owing to enemy action, John F Mallon
    Collection
Imperial War Museum Interview Sound Recording Catalogue
    Number 11963, Henderson, Hardie Mann Blatchford
Talk given by William Wells-Hood to the York Railway Lecture &
    Debating Society, 1921
Results of Inquiry into the circumstances of an accident at Littleburn
    on 21st December 1914, Board of Trade, 4th March 1915
Results of Inquiry into the circumstances of an accident at
    Scarborough on 17th March 1915, Board of Trade, 9th April 1915
Results of Inquiry into the circumstances of an accident at Chaloner
    Whin on 18th March 1915, Board of Trade, 22nd April 1915
Results of Inquiry into the circumstances of an accident at Micklefield
    on 9th December 1915, Board of Trade, 11th December 1915
Results of Inquiry into the circumstances of an accident at St Bede's
    Junction on 17th December 1915, Board of Trade, 3rd February
    1916
Results of Inquiry into the circumstances of an accident at
    Scremerston on 19th May 1916, Board of Trade, 9th June 1916
Results of Inquiry into the circumstances of an accident at Alne on
    19th December 1917, Board of Trade, 16th January 1918
Results of Inquiry into the circumstances of an accident between
    Newby Wiske and Sinderby stations on 15th April 1918, Board of
    Trade, 8th May 1918